## Praise for *Invisible Martyrs*

"Distorting the teachings of religion is not unique to extreme Islam in our time. We find it everywhere, and we all need to address it if we are to mend our world, which is undergoing a deep moral crisis. This book focuses on women who are recruited by radical organizations that distort the teaching of Islam. I share the author's conclusion that, as we have always seen in the past, those who have no regard for human life cannot succeed. The teachings of compassion and justice shared by all the major faiths will continue to prevail."
**—Rabbi Mordecai Schreiber**

"Farhana Qazi continues to serve as an ambassador between religions and cultures in difficult and violent times. Her book is a must-read to separate the peaceful practice of Islam from violent extremism."
**—Ambassador Akbar Ahmed, Ibn Khaldun Chair of Islamic Studies, American University**

"Farhana Qazi focuses on the importance of going local as the foundation for countering and preventing violent extremism, understanding that Muslims are the front line in the global war on terrorism."
**—Stephen M. Apatow, President, Humanitarian Resource Institute**

"Farhana Qazi highlights the precious gift of Islam in this book, which is to bring the misguided female extremist closer to the truth and understand a religion of love and mercy."
**—Jennifer Sue Parker, senior commander, US military**

"Farhana Qazi takes the reader on a well-written and analytically sharp tour of the world of women who kill in the name of God."
**—Peter Bergen, Vice President, New America Foundation, and National Security Analyst, CNN**

"Farhana Qazi's new book, *Invisible Martyrs*, is an authentic revelation of how Islam can be skewed by some, thus distorting the core fundamental goodness of the faith of Islam, and especially for gender issues. In this complex and volatile world, women reject terrorism and conflict—they search for peace, justice, and rights. Bravo to Farhana with this most important message in her new book."
**—Lois A. Herman, Coordinator, Women's UN Report Network**

"Informed by her own experience and personal encounters, Qazi's book takes us inside the mindset of those who, contrary to their own religious beliefs and to society's perceptions of women as nurturers, instead become its murderous fanatics. While avoiding the alarmist prose and political agendas that color so much of the literature on terrorism, *Invisible Martyrs* offers a fascinating and harrowing story. Of all the recent books on this topic, this one is an essential read."
**—Brian Michael Jenkins, Senior Adviser, RAND Corporation**

"Qazi has given us a deeply personal yet acutely analytical journey into the minds of the women and girls who seek out violent extremism. *Invisible Martyrs* is an electrifying page-turner that should be read by everyone who wants to understand this disturbing phenomenon."
**—John Horgan, senior counterterrorism adviser to the United States and Professor, Georgia State University**

"Qazi gives us a book that is bold, brave, and brilliant. A must-read for everyone trying to unpack violent extremism from a peaceful religion."
**—Amanda Ohlke, Adult Education Director, International Spy Museum**

"*Invisible Martyrs* reflects Qazi's personal spiritual journey as a Muslim American woman, mother, immigrant, and scholar trying to understand motives for terrorism that are so alien to her experiences with Islam. An antidote to complaints in the media that Muslims aren't speaking up, the book demonstrates that many Muslim scholars continue to be doing their part to combat what the author characterizes as a 'disturbing trend of an uncompromising Islamic scholarship spreading in the Muslim and Western world.' Qazi also suggests alternative narratives against extremism, in which struggling 'in the way of God' means taking the path to love, not to war."
**—Barbara Sude, former senior counterterrorism analyst, US government**

"Through storytelling, Qazi takes a deeper look at what motivates women and girls to join a dangerous and radical movement. This book is essential for anyone hoping to understand the dark truth of violent extremism as well as the beauty of Islam."
**—Angelina Maldonado, world affairs instructor**

"Farhana Qazi has utilized a lifetime of studying Islam to craft a book that sheds light on a great mystery. She comes at the subject as a scholar and an American woman who spent time with Muslim women to understand their motivations. Her insights are unique. She draws on a tremendous amount of research and reflection. It is a valuable read to help understand what Islam really says and how we might prevent future violence."
**—Vicky Collins, television producer and journalist**

"Compellingly written and hard to put down, Farhana Qazi's first-person perspective asks difficult questions about faith and culture while shining a light on an often-unexpected and unseen side of radical Islam."
—**Eric Tipton, author and screenwriter**

"With *Invisible Martyrs*, Farhana Qazi turns conventional thinking upside down and forces us to ask new questions about who engages in political violence and why. A highly original, compelling, and very readable exploration of a side of terrorism we know very little about."
—**Peter Mandaville, Professor of International Affairs and Islamic Studies, George Mason University, and former Senior Adviser to Secretaries of State Hillary Clinton and John Kerry**

"In her book, Qazi fights violent extremists by trying to capture the true spirit of Islamic teachings while also understanding and offering solutions to vulnerable Muslims who need to reject such messages and once again embrace a religion of peace."
—**Anne Speckhard, Director, International Center for the Study of Violent Extremism, and Adjunct Associate Professor of Psychiatry, Georgetown University School of Medicine**

"Farhana Qazi tells the fascinating inside story of the women who are ready to die for radical Islam."
—**Deborah Scroggins, author of *Wanted Women***

"Heartbreaking. The balance Qazi brings to a difficult story—extremism versus the teachings of peace and love—makes for a powerful read. Telling the story through the eyes of women makes it memorable."
—**Betsy Ashton, author and former President, Virginia Writers Club**

"With her inimitable insights, compelling analysis, and clear-eyed stories, Farhana Qazi makes a world opaque to most all of us accessible and vivid. This book has much for those willing to be taught and should be read widely."
—**Eric Selbin, Chair of International Studies, Professor of Political Science, and Lucy King Brown Chair, Southwestern University**

"Gripping. Lyrical. With *Invisible Martyrs*, Qazi tells stories that need to be heard and penetrates minds that need to be understood."
—**Ajit Maan, President, Narrative Strategies, and author of *Narrative Warfare***

"Qazi is a daring researcher who provides answers to why women and girls join extremism. With an open heart, she weaves in her own personal story to tell the world that ignorance of faith disempowers Muslim females. This is the only book by an American Muslim woman with a counterterrorism background that has the power to change hearts and minds."
—**Judit Maull, Producer, Happy Madison Productions**

"Farhana Qazi's courage and compassion inform this extraordinary book, which gives new and important insights into the radicalization of violent extremists. A beautifully crafted cri de coeur, *Invisible Martyrs* stands as crucial reading for all who share the author's dedication to freedom, security, human rights, and human dignity."

**—Abigail R. Esman, award-winning journalist, author, and member of Scholars for Peace in the Middle East**

# INVISIBLE MARTYRS

# INVISIBLE MARTYRS

*Inside the Secret World*
*of Female Islamic Radicals*

**Farhana Qazi**

**BK**

Berrett–Koehler Publishers, Inc.
*a BK Currents book*

Berrett-Koehler Publishers, Inc.
1333 Broadway, Suite 1000
Oakland, CA 94612-1921
Tel: (510) 817-2277
Fax: (510) 817-2278
www.bkconnection.com

**ORDERING INFORMATION**
*Quantity sales.* Special discounts are available on quantity purchases by corporations, associations, and others. For details, contact the "Special Sales Department" at the Berrett-Koehler address above.
*Individual sales.* Berrett-Koehler publications are available through most bookstores. They can also be ordered directly from Berrett-Koehler: Tel: (800) 929-2929; Fax: (802) 864-7626; www.bkconnection.com.
*Orders for college textbook / course adoption use.* Please contact Berrett-Koehler: Tel: (800) 929-2929; Fax: (802) 864-7626.

Distributed to the U.S. trade and internationally by Penguin Random House Publisher Services.

Berrett-Koehler and the BK logo are registered trademarks of Berrett-Koehler Publishers, Inc.

Printed in the United States of America

Berrett-Koehler books are printed on long-lasting acid-free paper. When it is available, we choose paper that has been manufactured by environmentally responsible processes. These may include using trees grown in sustainable forests, incorporating recycled paper, minimizing chlorine in bleaching, or recycling the energy produced at the paper mill.

**Library of Congress Cataloging-in-Publication Data**
Names: Qazi, Farhana, author.
Title: Invisible martyrs : inside the secret world of female Islamic radicals / Farhana Qazi.
Description: First Edition. | Oakland, CA : Berrett-Koehler Publishers, 2018.
Identifiers: LCCN 2018011562 | ISBN 9781626567900 (paperback)
Subjects: LCSH: Women terrorists--Islamic countries. | Women radicals--Islamic countries. | Islamic fundamentalism. | BISAC: POLITICAL SCIENCE / Political Freedom & Security / Terrorism. | SOCIAL SCIENCE / Women's Studies. | SOCIAL SCIENCE / Islamic Studies.
Classification: LCC HV6433.I74 Q39 2018 | DDC 363.325088/297082--dc23
LC record available at https://lccn.loc.gov/2018011562

**First Edition**
26 25 24 23 22 21 20 19 18          10 9 8 7 6 5 4 3 2 1

*Book producer:* Linda Jupiter Productions   *Cover designer:* Paula Goldstein
*Editor:* Elissa Rabellino                          *Proofreader:* Mary Kanable
*Text designer:* Morning Hullinger,             *Indexer:* Paula C. Durbin-Westby
    The Color Mill

*To my teachers*

"Whoever saves one life, saves all of humanity."

—THE QURAN 5:32

"Those who are merciful will be shown mercy by the Most Merciful. Be merciful to those on the earth and the One above the heavens will have mercy upon you."

—MUHAMMAD, the Prophet of Islam

# CONTENTS

# FOREWORD

Farhana Qazi is a gifted storyteller. Her ability to bring her readers into the heads and hearts of her subjects is remarkable. Once my favorite graduate student, she is now a treasured colleague with whom I have coauthored several articles, blending her cultural sensitivity with my focus on psychobiography, personality, and trauma. In all of our work together, the sum is greater than the parts.

In her work to make the motivations of terrorists, especially female terrorists, comprehensible, Farhana relies on her gifted interviewing skills. She manages to make the life stories of her subjects vital and compelling. There is but a small number of terrorism scholars who rely on sensitive interviews to make their subjects come alive. Thus Farhana's superb storytelling ability, as reflected in her fine book, *Invisible Martyrs*, helps shine a light that illuminates what makes terrorists tick and that emphasizes well the increasingly mainstream role of female terrorists.

Increasingly, as Farhana demonstrates, Muslim women are not merely playing a supportive role but are becoming active participants in terrorist attacks, a kind of equal employment opportunity among radical Muslim women. She recounts her lonely road as the first Muslim woman to work in the U.S. government's Counterterrorism Center. She describes her painful path in confronting her own Muslim faith, seeing that it was not only the warm and loving faith with which she had grown up—that the verses of the Quran could be used by radical Muslims to justify violence.

History is rapidly changing. The major terrorism scholar David Rapoport, in reviewing terrorist history, has identified four terrorist waves: the anarchist wave, the nationalist-separatist wave, the social-revolutionary wave, and the religious extremist wave. While we are still immersed in the religious extremist wave, there is now a wave so powerful that it merits being identified as the fifth wave: the social media wave.

Social media is increasingly associated with being radicalized online, and for women, the electronic medium can be very attractive. It is also attractive to lone-wolf terrorists. No longer isolated and alone, they have access to the virtual community of hatred, and this is an extremely difficult counterterrorism challenge.

Farhana has found Islam through her counterterrorism work and believes that a pure and peaceful practice of the faith can help vulnerable women and girls say no to violent extremism. Her enduring belief in love, mercy, and tolerance is the guiding light for this memorable book.

Jerrold Post, MD, PhD
April 2018

# AUTHOR'S NOTE

*This is a true story.* Everything in this book happened. Over the past few years, the vast majority of terrorist attacks happened on our television screens or the public places we go to. What we did not see in media reports is recorded in this book: the hundreds of women and their children who joined terrorist groups, as well as the hundreds more who dared to stand against terrorists to protect their families and communities. Women who speak up face numerous death threats. Therefore, some interviews are compressed, having taken place over multiple meetings. Some portions are not presented in the exact order of actual events. There are no composite characters; there are only sensitive sources and some people who wish to be unnamed and unknown to the public. Due to safety concerns, some names have been changed, and in some special cases (as clearly noted in the text), details of context were omitted. Ultimately, this is a personal story inside the dark world of terrorists and the survivors of war.

# PREFACE

My first day at the Counterterrorism Center began with a bombing. In October 2000, al-Qaeda killed seventeen American sailors and injured nearly forty when a small boat carrying explosives crashed into a US Navy destroyer, the USS *Cole*, in Yemen's Aden harbor. This was the deadliest attack against an American ship since 1987, when an Iraqi jet aircraft fired missiles at the USS *Stark*.

Men and women clad in business suits ran down the hallway. Everyone headed to the same large conference room. When the director, Cofer Black, entered, there was silence.

"We have been hit," he said.

*We are at war with al-Qaeda—an enemy we don't understand.*

In my mid-twenties, I was one of the youngest counterterrorism analysts and the first Muslim female to join the center. I knew I had much to learn. The daily dose of intelligence was mind-numbing. I memorized facts and details by keeping a dossier of terrorist attacks and tried to make my own predictions. Al-Qaeda attacked the World Trade Center in 1993. Would it do that again? In summer 1998, two US embassies in Africa were struck the same day. Could multipronged attacks signal a new tactic? In 2002, Wafa Idris became the first female Palestinian suicide bomber when she detonated a twenty-two-pound bomb in Jerusalem and killed more than one hundred people. Were women the new stealth bomb?

The bombing of the USS *Cole* proved that Muslim terrorists could take the world by surprise by conducting an attack in the most unpredictable place with an unimaginable tactic. Identifying radical men—and later women—who acted in the name of Islam forced me to reexamine my faith. Unfortunately, there was no one with whom I could discuss the tenets of Islam or radical Islam and make sense of intelligence reporting. I was the *first* American Muslim in the center, so I had to rely on my own knowledge of Islamic literature, history, and scripture to explain—or not explain—the use of violence by radicalized Muslims.

Tracking terrorists was unlike anything I knew how to do. I had no role model and no mentor, only my trusted friend Sara. There were no savvy spy scholars in the building, and certainly no Muslim intellectuals I could lean on to explain the perversion of Islam. I am reminded of the film *The Recruit*, in which the CIA instructor played by Al Pacino tells a class of young recruits, "Trust yourself." For as long as I worked in the center, I had no one but myself to lean on. I knew I had to persuade and prevail in an environment where intolerance and ignorance of my faith existed. I had a great deal of work ahead of me to convince my colleagues and managers of the beauty *within* Islam; the majority of Muslims believe in dialogue and nonviolent protest to oppose war, conflict, and crimes committed against Muslims.

At the time, given the nature of our work and the around-the-clock schedule of monitoring threats, it was nearly impossible to develop a mentoring program to guide a new hire. Luckily, I had an *outside* mentor for life, Dr. Jerrold Post, a prominent psychiatrist known for profiling hostile leaders, including the late demagogues Saddam Hussein of Iraq and Libya's Muammar Gaddafi. Dr. Post showed me, through case studies and his own interviews of terrorists, that they could also be heartbreakingly human: terrorists may have loved and lost; they may have been troubled children or traumatized adults; and their disconnectedness from life led them to constantly push for survival and sanity. He taught me what I always believed: that radical Muslims chose suicidal death in the form of what they considered to be labeled martyrdom operations as the answer to restorative justice because they believed it was the way into the Afterlife. While committing to the cause in *this* life, but focused on Paradise, terrorists were reborn—the Afterlife was their quantum leap.

As much as I admired Dr. Post, he could not tell me about the secret world I was about to enter, except that I belonged at the center. "They need someone with your knowledge of Islam. If there's anyone who can understand, it's you," he said. He graced me with his gentleness and gifted me his understanding, and decades of real research, on Muslim terrorists.

Inside the center, I led a bizarre life. I learned the tradecraft and skills that would serve me well after leaving the US government. I traveled to foreign cities and met people whom I never would have known, had I chosen a normal nine-to-five day job in the private sector, at a think tank, or at a newspaper.

Working in the center taught me a valuable lesson: *Nothing is as it seems.* In those early years, I was haunted by visions of being followed. I often looked over my shoulder. I minced my words when speaking with family members and relatives, including those who had become naturalized Americans. I was on the constant lookout for anything or anyone suspicious—my life revolved around the idea that *our enemies are everywhere.*

From the inside of my cubicle, the dark and disturbing world of religious extremism defied everything I had been taught about Islam and contradicted what I had seen of *good* Muslim women and their men. I had not considered that seemingly pious Muslim women, with or without the *hijab* (veil), would support extremist men or strap on the suicide belt, which meant leaving a family behind—in Islam, a woman's first responsibility *is* her family, not the terrorist organization she joins. I had never considered that a Muslim woman could be as absurdly daring, deceiving, and deranged as male terrorists. Nor had I foreseen that Muslim women with children could impugn their gender and destroy families with senseless acts of violence.

I had always believed that women everywhere were nurturers of their society. Many women raised children and worked; others simply worked. Whatever their choices, women were symbols of strength and love. Nothing about a woman wearing a bomb, encouraging her men to be terrorists, or publishing violent poetry made her compassionate, even when she claimed to be supporting violence so that future generations of children could live. That argument rarely persuaded moderate Muslims to join a violent cause or organization.

During my career, the appearance of names of radical Muslim women on my computer screen compelled me to report them to the White House and other senior officials in the US government.

I needed to warn the officials. I drafted an intelligence assessment with the catchy title, "From Rocking the Cradle to Rocking the World: Why Muslim Women Kill," which I published in an international women's journal when the original report was declassified in 2005.

But the early warnings did not change policy. In those early days, there were too few extremist women to justify initiating dramatic change or transforming the way we collected and analyzed intelligence—until the question of female detainees was raised. One morning, a government psychiatrist asked me to write an instructional guide on how to treat captured Muslim women.

"We have to be prepared," she said. "We need to know what to do, and you can help us."

*Because I am Muslim? Because I know what a violent Muslim woman looks like? Because I know what a female terrorist is thinking when she commits or supports terrorism? Or maybe you think I can stop these women with Islamic scripture?* I had not contemplated what I might do if actually faced with a female terrorist, a psychopath who shared my faith.

Before I began my work in the center, I had known the ugly truth. The pages of history are filled with violent acts committed by women from different religious traditions. They have been responsible for terrible crimes: fratricide, infanticide, serial murder, torture, massacres, judicial murder, and suicide terrorism—a relatively new form of violence committed by radical men and the women who join them.

Statistically, however, women are not the deadlier sex. Women represent less than 2 percent of the world's serial killers, and today's female suicide bombers are a small fraction of bombers. So unusual are Muslim female terrorists that they are vilified for committing the type of crime that men are most likely to commit but also for the fact of being female. How could a woman have done such a terrible thing? For years, I have had to address this simple question with complex answers, harking back to my government service that changed the way I looked at love's martyrs—females dying for a cause, community, country, and more. Their death was an assault on my religion.

Before 9/11, the mission was simple and clear: find terrorists and ascertain their motives, messages, and multiple networks of support. This is what I had been trained to do. In the center, I was labeled *the* Islam expert by some. Analysts and managers asked me questions about doctrine. Some questioned Islam itself. Others mocked my religion and conflated it with radical Islam. *If we are going to defeat religious extremism, we need to learn how they think.* Each day, I reminded myself that the center chose me, the Punjabi girl from Texas, to help fight the enemies of America. While serving my country, I had a more personal reason for staying in the center: I wanted to prove that Islam is a religion of peace, mercy, and compassion; that radical women (and men) destroyed the teachings of Islam by recreating scripture through visions of death and false promises of glory for the martyrs in love with a flight to Heaven.

Within a short time, I earned a reputation and recognition for my service, answering the late-night phone call and skipping family events to piece together intelligence assessments for the President's Daily Brief. Those were the days when all I could say with confidence was, "This might happen." Too many probabilities clouded in uncertainty. My secret obsession then and for years to come was to write, think, and lecture on the future—that is, the unexpected—role of radical women as they made that journey into the labyrinth of death.

*Why do some women kill?* That one simple question by a senior US government official would consume me my entire career.

# AWAKENING

For years, I dreamed of hijackings on airplanes. In my dreams, men with dark eyes wore black masks and wielded sharp weapons. They spoke a language I vaguely understood and made plans to strike a passenger. At that moment, I rose from my seat to announce my faith: "*La illaha illa la Muhammadan rasulilah.*" ("There is no God but God and Muhammad is His Prophet.") I said it three times. The masked men stopped. They looked at each other. They didn't know what to say or do. I clutched the scarf I had pulled out of my handbag and recited the first lines in the Quran, "The Opening Verse." The men remained standing, motionless, until someone said in Gulf-accented Arabic, "Who are you?"

In the dreams, Sara was always next to me. We have been together for as long as I can remember. We went to the same college in Texas, overlooking hill country, and then I followed her to the same graduate school in Washington, DC. We both joined the Counterterrorism Center. We have so much in common: we love to travel to the Middle East, write and speak on foreign policy issues, and learn foreign languages—Sara mastered Pashto, the tongue of the Afghans—and we both love mint tea. If I had a blond-haired sister, it would be Sara. Which is why I'm not surprised that she is always with me in the hijacking dream or when I have terrible visions of being kidnapped by masked murderers—all of whom are Muslim—and I pretend to be the Muslim heroine by saving Sara.

Looking back, I know that the dark dreams forced me to focus on the mission. Each morning, I donned a business suit and gold jewelry and drove twenty minutes from my home to Langley, Virginia. The guards looked the same. The glass building glinted in the morning light. My key card, which let me through security and into my vaulted office, had the same royal blue background with a younger-looking me—an innocent version of myself when I had just embarked on the career that would change and challenge me in unimaginable ways.

On most days, when Sara was not traveling overseas, we would talk about our lives. Our parents were in Texas—her family lived in Houston, and my parents had lived in the same house in Austin for more than thirty years. She asked me about my baby boy. I began my career as a young mother at the age of twenty-five. We talked about our work too—the terrorists' profiles and the countries where the men were from. Before 9/11, intelligence analysts investigated mostly men because women were largely invisible; we later learned that women would play a vital role in terrorist organizations as supporters, sympathizers, and staunch loyalists. Few women would commit suicide attacks.

We exchanged stories on the places we visited and the police officers, security personnel, and government elites we met in foreign countries. We treasured the gifts we gave to one another. During her trip to Israel, Sara took a picture of Al-Aqsa Mosque in Jerusalem, a holy city where Muslims believe Prophet Muhammad ascended to Heaven to speak to God. Years later, she gifted me "The Verse of the Throne," known as *Ayatul Kursi*, written in large golden letters on black cloth sealed in a golden-glass frame.

When we worked together, Sara and I shared our secrets. She helped me, a young Muslim woman. What she couldn't do was help me understand Islam and provide answers to questions that I asked every time Muslims perpetrated a terrorist attack: Why do Muslims commit violence in the name of their religion? What does Islam say about jihad? And why am I the *only* Muslim woman here?

For years, I listened, learned, and lived with the words spoken by violent extremists. When the voices of terrorists haunted my dreams, and nights became hallucinatory, I found comfort in the silence of open spaces: the solitude of faith inside an empty mosque, deep evergreen forests and the blue waters of Dal Lake in my grandmother's homeland, the fields of golden brown in a Texan summer, a long road cobbled with shrubs and threaded with wandering tree roots in northern Pakistan, and the red barn situated on land with plum trees and grazed by horses that I loved as a child in Tennessee, my first American home before moving to Texas. The person I used to be longed for order—a child with a memory of fleeting images and faith in the benevolent blue sky of the American Southwest wanted the world to remain blue, green, translucent; as Henry David Thoreau said, "All good things are wild and free."

Even as I tried to forget the attacks by Muslims and the images of death and destruction they caused, the actions of a radical few evoked an endless torrent of rage that kept alive a cacophony of voices inside my head, warning me to fight back—as a Muslim, a woman, and an American. It was overwhelming. No one taught me how to stay strong or how to hide my fury toward our enemies. No one helped me to overcome my awkwardness when probed by members of my faith-based community about what I did and where I worked. Quietly, I covered my agitation and survived those early years as a woman on edge—always waiting for the next attack.

I remembered a prayer that my mother chanted when she first experienced the ugliness of war in her birth country of Pakistan: *Be constantly occupied with listening to God. Believe that He has a purpose for you.* The only way I knew how to deal with difficulties, such as the allegation that Islam is a violent faith, was to surrender my happiness to the clarity that came from a daily practice of Islam: a simple hum at the break of dawn, the memory of serene mosques surrounded by gardens and huge rectangular pools, and an unmoved conviction in poetry.

As I learned more about Islam, I also began to look deeply at the profiles of terrorist women. The oft-repeated question of why they did it forced me to look beyond the "push and pull" drivers of violent extremism. I had to humanize the girls and women who committed savage crimes. I had to admit to myself that not all violent women were delusional, disturbed, depressed, or distracted—that they could be rational too. I had to find a way to know *them*, the women of terror, if I was going to understand a life broken by death—a world surreal to me but real and romantic to them. Perhaps they were trapped in an endless dream, imagining a paradisiacal place with pink clouds and the intensity of light defined as the touch of God.

In time, the agonizing dreams stopped. I did not see Sara or myself captured, tortured, or, worse, raped by maniacs shouting religious verse. Images perceived between light and shadow diminished. The deathbed colors of nighttime visions faded, and I suspect that my original desire to be a Muslim heroine in the face of terror drifted as soon as I realized that there was another way to save myself from the tormentors.

When the nightmares subsided, I could see beyond the fragmented conversations of masked men who came to me as apparitions. I could see that my faith was meant to be simple, rational, and practical. Islam is a clear and simple faith, not a complex set of beliefs and principles that reserve Paradise for the chosen few. I realized that terrorists dismissed a history of compassion and mercy preached by the prophets and messengers sent by God.

In my search for the truth, I would listen to saints and study the teachings of Islam, trying to understand why extremists distorted the faith. In time, I would learn how to distinguish between legitimate and illegitimate reasons for taking up arms and the role of Muslim women in conflict. After leaving the US government and in the years to come, I would give lectures on Muslim responses to violence, telling stories with statistical proof that the majority of Muslims believe in and live by the Prophet's earlier *hadith*, or oral tradition: "Those who are merciful will be shown mercy by the Most Merciful. Be merciful to those on the earth, and the One above the heavens will have mercy upon you."

To crush extremism, I preached what I believed to be true: that a *lived* Islam is the answer to violent extremism and today's increasing far-right-wing movement. Earlier messengers taught me that a practice of self-awareness, self-devotion, and a selflessness that honors God and the country I call home is founded on the principle of mercy—the attribute that enables people to replace bigotry with benevolence, prejudice with patience, and chauvinism with consent. If there's anything I've learned from my counterterrorism work, it is that extremism of any kind expunges clarity, charity, and compassion from citizenry.

Undoubtedly, violent extremism is one of the most complex subjects of the modern century. The reasons why women commit acts of violence are multifaceted. The diversity of Muslim women is often explained in extreme contrast: modernity and antiquity, luxury and poverty, sensuality and asceticism, tenderness and violence; a multiplicity of cultures, clans, families, and tribes describe the "Muslim woman." She is a product of local cultures, traditions, histories, and politics. In this book of stories and prose, even violent Muslim women are more than the constructs of patriarchal practice or norms codified by men.

This book is about what happened when I discovered Islam through the women who distorted it with violence, as they helped me untangle and unravel the tenets of my faith. Through them, I found best practices and policies to counter violent extremism. I discovered intervention strategies that are slowly helping women hold on to faith as they struggle with versions of orthodox Islam polluted by extremist interpretations. And in the process, I discovered a gentle Islam and more about myself as a woman of faith.

The more I studied violent women, the more I realized that there were multiple, if not parallel, realities, and the best I could hope for was a near-complete story of the women who kill. Trying to figure out the motives of female killers was an addiction, and I was badly hooked. So this is how I began this book: with the belief that the ink of the scholar is mightier than the blood of the sword, an Islamic teaching posted on the wall of my office. As a Muslim woman with a counterterrorism background, I became obsessed with the question of *why now?* Why are some women drawn to violence? To find the answer, I started talking to women and their men. I listened to hundreds of people talk about their passage to God. Some chose the path of violence as they struggled with religion and identity, while other women offered solutions for peace and supported women's rights as a counter to violent men.

I believed I would find the answers to the questions that tormented my childhood and young adulthood if I entered the world of conflict to understand the rationale for extremism. Mine was a personal quest to find the larger, grander narratives of violence; the histories of beliefs contained within families; and the biographies of women that would be revealed in a language of song, verse, and metaphors. I had to accept the way in which stories were enfolded within other stories and learn to listen to the terrible, fatal truths in a time of war.

This book is personal because terrorism is personal. I learned this vital truth at home through the details of my mother's life in Pakistan described in chapter 1. Because Mama was willing to fight in a military uniform to free Kashmir, she was my first woman warrior. After I left home and joined the US government, I learned a great deal about women, young and old, willing to die for a cause. I drafted sketchy profiles of these early female terrorists in intelligence assessments for the White House, senior defense officials, and intelligence officers stationed overseas. But it was when I left the US government and traveled widely that I met with hundreds of people—both victims and perpetrators of violence—and came to understand that the whole language of terrorism has been corrupted by overuse. Their stories are laced throughout the book. I have learned to accept that each woman's story is unique and develops in a specific context, culture, and condition.

The more I listened, the more I observed the deeply personal arguments, incentives, and drivers for why some women choose violence or are coerced into violent extremism. I recognized that two people could speak of terrorism, and yet this concept might mean significantly different things for each person. So many people today don't know what terrorism is and engage in a battle of semantics instead of focusing on the root causes of violence or why terrorism begins, which is what I call *context*. As a former government analyst, I accepted the United States' oversimplified definition of terrorism as the use of violence by an individual or group to achieve a political goal. In truth, the politics of terrorists are connected to the religious language of the believer, who is committed to restoring an Islamic ideal throughout the world.

I learned that the intimate details of an extremist's life are the story of life and death. Recruits are told allegories of the forever and glorious Afterlife, a Paradise promised to the most honorable of women and men. It's the story told by the female propagandist proving the existence of God by exposing her own deep, sad wounds; or by the women, wishing to be soothed by love, who join a savage war to rebel against real and perceived enemies. Lost in the stories of amoral actions intended by violent women is the unspeakable beauty of victims who live on in the memories of survivors.

What is the allure of extremism? In my lectures, I emphasize culture, context, and capability, what I call the Three Cs. In the world of counterterrorism, a neat arrangement of "root causes" allows authorities and experts to engage directly with the problem. The trouble is, this complex phenomenon needs to be properly identified and understood before intervention begins, because the solution to countering violent extremism, or CVE, is not always clean, clear, or uncomplicated.

*Culture.* Across time and conflicts, women who opt for or are selected for violence accept strongly held beliefs and religious rights. Every Muslim culture has its own norms and customs for its women. In some societies, men's attitudes about women's rights are extreme examples of control, creating a cultural chasm of gender rights. In various cultures, what women can and can't do is often dictated by men. As this book reveals, male terrorist leaders who extolled female martyrs had specific gains (often, male extremists use women to advance their cause and ensure their own survival), which had nothing to do with granting women positions of power.

The same was true of Palestinian female operatives who strapped on the bomb before men encouraged women to die for the cause in Iraq: The earlier examples of Palestinian girls and women who detonated bombs in Israel proved that prevailing conservatives in the Middle East were willing to compromise their Islamic orthodoxy if the female bomber and supporters of violence advanced the vested interests of men. Chapter 3, "Deception," on Iraq, exposes the culture of violence manipulated by men to invite women into suicide terrorism and explains why it worked until it didn't.

In other Muslim cultures, a woman's taking on the role of a man can be perceived as shameful to a man's pride and ego. This partly explains why so few female bombers have surfaced in Afghanistan,

Pakistan, or the valley of Kashmir—none of these places have a history of female suicide terrorism, and the few attacks perpetrated by women are an exception, not the standard. When I was a senior instructor on the Afghanistan-Pakistan Regional Training Team, teaching the US military about Islam and the prevailing culture, I explained in a seminar on radical women why most men in this region do not choose women for violent attacks: men believe they are the sole guardians of women, preserving deeply traditional gender roles; men shield women from public life, defending local customs that divide men and women into specific spaces; and because men view their honor through their women, they guard them like their swords or ancient relics, which means that women are viewed by some men as property.

In Afghanistan and Pakistan, where culture trumps religion, there are few cases of female terrorists. And there is no history of girls dying in Kashmir on a suicide mission. But there are numerous cases of women marrying would-be martyrs, women willing to be made widows for the terrorist group to which they belong. This book includes the story of an accidental meeting with a young woman who volunteered for a suicide mission because she believed this was the only way to call attention to the conflict in Kashmir.

**Context.** Like culture, contextual pressures help explain radical behavior. These pressures can be personal or political and are often labeled as "push and pull" factors for radicalization, which include gross human rights violations, widespread corruption, poorly governed areas, and the presence of protracted local conflicts.[1] Recently there have been several high-profile cases of young women from the West turning to terrorism online, a new phenomenon that Dr. Post calls the "virtual community of hatred." Terrorism experts are asking: What do these girls want? Why is this happening? And how can we stop it? Several motives seem likely: to help other Muslims in need, an unequivocal love and desire for unconditional acceptance, a fixed identity that is true to Islam, a twisted Islamic feminism, and many more. Reports published by the Institute for Strategic Dialogue on the girls of ISIS provide some examples of women and girls who have traveled to Syria to find their fantastical forever male partner.

I have seen the sites where girls became instant BFFs (best friends forever) looking for love, family, meaning, identity, and maybe adventure. A girl using the moniker Umm Musa (or the "mother of Moses") titled her Twitter page "'Til Martyrdom Do Us Part," with a picture of herself in all-black clothing with a red band across her forehead containing Arabic letters. She, like other girls, maintained her anonymity online, calling herself a *mujahidah* ("female fighter"). In the book *Women, Gender, and Terrorism*, I contributed a chapter on the first female fighters in early Islam—the women who stood by their messenger in seventh-century Arabia.[2] These women had nothing in common with contemporary radicals disguised as fighters—some with weapons slung across their shoulders, others aspiring to be the "housewives of Raqqa" and mothers of future fighters for a mythical Caliphate.

Using the Internet, females are accessible and available to ISIS men. A French girl posing as Mélodie, a twenty-year-old woman, proved how easy it is to find radicals online. Within hours of creating her profile, she began chatting with a man named Bilel, who insisted on giving his cyber-sweetheart a new Islamic name. In her gripping memoir, *Undercover Jihadi Bride*, Anna Erelle wrote, "The identity change that Bilel demanded affected me. Day by day, he was psychologically killing Mélodie. She had to sacrifice everything for him; her life, her past, her mother, everybody she loved, and now this, the one thing that remained of her origins: her first name."[3]

Mélodie was an impostor posing as a "jihadi bride"; Muslim girls who are connected to ISIS men online agree to and accept the new identity, the new name, the new place. Bilel declared to Mélodie, "My life, my wife, from now on, you will be called Umm Saladine. Welcome to the true Islam." The same held true for hundreds of girls in the West, including teenagers in the American Southwest who almost made it to Syria because they wanted a new version of themselves. Girls wanting to shed their family, friends, and past can start a new life. These girls are committed believers, choosing a perverted Islam that contradicts the true practice of Islam. Their version of faith dilutes the principles of peace, love, and mercy preached by the Prophet of Islam and practiced by millions of Muslims today. This book includes the story of the Denver girls who were lured by radical men on the Internet to go to Syria and were on their way there when they were found and returned to their families. Had they reached Syria, it's almost certain that these girls would never have been found.

*Capability.* The final C is related to competence. The story of the famed female shooter in San Bernardino in December 2015 proved that she had had training. When she gunned down fourteen people at a community center, it was clear that she knew how to fire a weapon; she knew whom to marry to enter the United States; and she understood the importance of hiding her identity and dark intentions. Tashfeen Malik had a plan, and leaving behind her six-month-old baby was part of the strategy. Maybe Malik knew she would be killed by authorities in a deadly shootout for the crime she was about to commit, and she was prepared to die. The husband-and-wife team is a relatively new form of terrorism and has been labeled lone-wolf attackers. I can only presume that Malik and her husband, Syed Farook, believed that they didn't need a team of killers. Two people were capable of committing mayhem, murder, and a massacre. More would just get in her way. After all, she proved herself capable, and that's all that mattered.

In truth, few experts have captured the suffering, sacrifice, or survival of women in conflict. By highlighting culture, context, and capability, I have tried to clearly explain why women become involved in terrorism. I know that the Three Cs is anything but an all-inclusive model, and it may appear limited by other macro-level root causes. Even as I write this, there is no absolute guide to the drivers of violent extremism. There are public studies and labyrinthine reports, and intelligence assessments I once used to write. Early on, I recognized that examining the unclassified world of Muslim women is the most effective way to understand the tangled world of radicals, both active and passive supporters of violence.

In her seminal and prize-winning book *Shoot the Women First* (1992), journalist Eileen MacDonald argued that women are more violent than men. Her stories rattled my belief in women's gifted ability to nurture and care for their family, community, and country. When I discovered her work, the thought of a woman strapping on the suicide belt or supporting a terrorist group couched in Islamic rhetoric and imagery stunned me, as it did most law-abiding, peace-loving Muslims. I was unprepared for what I would find as a researcher-storyteller: that a Muslim woman could inflict harm on other Muslims and non-Muslims, that there was no easy way to identify femmes fatales and their supporters, and that violent women use Islamic text and symbolism to restore justice in an unjust war. The latter unnerved me for a long time because "violent *jihad*" is against the principles, values, and traditions of Islam.

No Muslim woman has the right to choose death over life. Muslims believe that death is not a destined choice. Only God determines our final hour. The Quran, Islam's holy book, and multiple sayings of the Prophet forbid suicide. If religion is unambiguous on prohibitions against suicide—and, by extension, suicide terrorism—why do women choose to die? Why do women justify a sin so clearly forbidden by the Prophet of Islam? In a famous tradition, Muhammad said, "The gates of Heaven are forever closed to anyone who takes his [or her] own life." Only God has the right to choose a person's time of death.

In my professional life, I continued to search for Islam's purpose and the "rightful" place of its women. Writing about women in Islam, and by extension, extremist women with a penchant for violence, opened up possibilities for greater understanding. I began to distinguish between the self-proclaimed "purist" and the betrayed believer trailing radical messages propagated by extremists. The violent visionaries came to me accidentally as their names were released in intelligence reporting, and later, in at-home or in-prison interviews. At the very least, women reveal their *intention* to conduct violence and/or join an extremist group, but few of them are accessible—they are in hiding and unreachable or unknown to the outside world—which makes it nearly impossible to discern the *beginning* of a woman's entrance into radical Islam.

Therein lies the great danger and dilemma for terrorism analysts. Without access, scholars and security officers turn to second-hand sources, sketching fragmented life histories. Over the years,

I have entered the homes of countless Muslim women, violent and nonviolent, searching for a true picture of who or what may influence, inspire, and induce women to action. Instead of the tired stereotype of the female terrorist "behind the veil," I have been looking for a more complete history, an expansive list of motives that can explain the behavior of women in, or deeply exposed to, conflict.

Like my contemporaries, I have resigned myself to the fact-as-observation that we will never know everything about female radicals. What I can do is provide thoughtful, never-before-told stories of women: some with massively defended psyches and cold, loveless smiles; others who are dissociated from what has happened to them in childhood or as young adults; the few with a world-weary attitude and an unreasoning desire to find Paradise that lingers long after; and women with the creative energy to remake the story of their life and change the status quo.

When I entered the private spaces of Muslim women, I discovered that some viewed violence as a weapon of choice. They believed in the radical interpretations of Islam. These women joined extremist groups to give purpose to their lives and effect change: to rewrite the future, to say *I am* within the boundaries set by men, to cleanse an unwanted past, to fall into favor with God, to cast away something broken or bruised or scraped, to push beyond the limits of their gender, to find a like-minded lover, or to experience the connection that a woman feels when she joins a sisterhood.

To be fair, this book is not everything you ever wanted to know about female terrorists or radical Islam. No book on this subject can be comprehensive for three reasons: First, the threat is evolving, and more women are joining (and recruiting other women) as I write this. Second, access to female terrorists is an ongoing challenge, which means the information we have on female radicals is sometimes cursory. For example, when a female extremist dies, we lose the ability to learn her intentions, motivations, and personal grievances. Instead, we piece together the lives of women, acting as a detective or an investigative journalist. When a female terrorist is captured, she is off-limits for national security reasons, except to a few journalists and terrorism analysts who are able to gain access and tell her story. Third, there is a growing body of literature found in online lectures and videos on radical Islam posted by non-Muslims, who are engaged in an open tug-of-war against peaceful, practicing Muslims that is contaminating the water of truth.

While the book's primary focus is on extremist women, the majority of Muslim women are *not* violent, and they are equally important to this story. Most Muslim women in the West and the Islamic world practice Islam peacefully; some of these women are fighting radical Islam on their own terms. They have created organizations and led movements to support women, calling for greater gender equality and education. There are also silent advocates who are not interested in gaining global attention for attacking zealots imposing unorthodox Islamic practice. With patience, perseverance, and prudence, a community of nonviolent Muslim women are guarding and guiding their faith.

Despite their extremes, terrorists give women a voice. They encourage women of all ages, including teenagers, to do something more than go to school, go to the mosque, or stay at home. Groups like ISIS, also known as ISIL, promise women an idyllic life beyond the celestial orbits of comets and asteroids not yet seen. Extremist men empower women with violent *fatwas*, or edicts, that fall outside the legal restrictions of Sharia or Islamic law. Men give women new identities, starting with a name, and help them leave behind families. Men convince some women of their right to choose suicide missions that they call martyrdom; radical men rescue females from a paroxysm of despair and promise marriage forever—a partner in this life and a lover for the Afterlife. These men recruit women using political statements, allowing women to believe they have joined a global movement, a fantastical nationhood ideal presented as the solution to all problems. By answering the call to conflict, these women lean toward a fragmented Islamic law, siding with ignominious orthodoxy as the defense of the Muslim community, and therefore these women lose their religious privileges: the Prophet of Islam advanced the status of women, which radical men today violate when they manipulate female recruits. The women's ignorance of authentic faith results in a series of terrible mistakes and useless victories in senseless wars.

The story begins at home.

Chapter One

# DESTINY

*Austin, Texas*

Growing up in Texas, I learned about war from my mother. I listened to stories of countries born out of conflict; women taking up arms for national pride; and the speeches, songs, and scholarship created by women to fight their oppressors. Mama taught me about female fighters. I was always curious about why she chose to join the army, why she rallied for a socialist political party, and how she lied to her family to do what she believed was her God-given right as a woman. *The right to go to war. The right to vote. And the right to choose her destiny.*

We lived on a quiet, tree-lined street in north Austin. I knew very little about the country of my birth, Pakistan, or the religion I was born into, Islam. On faith, Mama preached: *Pray when you can. Fast if you're healthy. Never judge anyone. Take care of the poor and your parents.* Islam was made simple and easy, so long as my sister and I followed the cultural traditions cloaked by religion.

When I was a girl, my mother introduced me to Kashmir, a place that bids fair to being Heaven on earth. A tiny fraction of the world's population lives in the blue-green hills, divided unevenly between the two nuclear-rival countries of India and Pakistan. More than ten million Kashmiris live on the Indian side and six million live in the autonomous territory of Pakistan. By contrast, my childhood home in the state of Texas is twice the size of all of Kashmir. This region is the site of the world's highest battlefield, at twenty thousand feet, where Indian and Pakistani military troops fought. Though Mama romanticized Kashmir, she had never visited or lived near the white-blue mountains. For her and millions of Pakistanis, the valley symbolized resistance.

"Kashmir is worth dying for," Mama said.

On September 6, 1965, Pakistani soldiers crossed the ceasefire line and entered Indian-controlled Kashmir. The army began looking for female recruits. My mother volunteered. "I was the only girl from a college of two hundred students to sign up for training," she boasted.

After class, Mama boarded a bus heading to the cricket stadium in Lahore, where the air swirled with dust and mosquitos. She slipped on her military uniform—a statement piece 100 percent her own—with her hazelnut-colored hair falling to her shoulders. She learned how to shoot the enemy. She learned how to load a British-style rifle known as the 303. She learned how to bandage a wounded soldier.

Mama trained without wearing the hijab or burqa, the head-to-ankle cloth that flowed loosely to hide the contours of a woman's body. Refusing to cover her hair, Mama reminded me of American women in jeans, a symbol of the sexual revolution in the 1960s. I remember thinking how bold and sanguine she was while growing up in a country that offered girls few choices. She valued her freedom and refused to be controlled or cajoled by men. Not even *her* mother believed in male dominance or the meddling of family members. "Independence is God's greatest gift to women," Nano would say.

At the outset, I had no idea that Mama's story of a time long gone, and fragments of the truth shrouded in mystery, would lead me to *other* women in war. True to her faith, Mama is thankful for what she did.

*Why did you want to fight?*

"I had hope for my country. I wanted to prove that women are capable of what men can do. Besides, men can't fight wars alone. They need women to help them," she said with her characteristic Punjabi bluntness.

"The only freedom I had was the freedom to fight."

Going to war for her country was Mama's jihad, her inner struggle to be true to herself. In Islam, the simple meaning of *jihad* is to strive and prevail over one's ego, or *nafs*. Listening to my mother's stories, I believed that she needed to fight to feel alive, to break free of all conventional rules, and to stand for a universal spirituality that welcomes women into God's kingdom. In a country beset with political disputes, endless power struggles, and religious clashes, Mama believed she could help Pakistan win the war.

Mama was caught up in patriotic fervor. Unlike most women of her time, she supported soldiers by wanting to go to battle. She was not the type of woman who would sew needed items or make bandages, though she did receive basic medical training. Mama reminded me of women I would read about as a teenager—the courageous women of the American Civil War, who defied society's expectations and bravely chose to take on more dangerous, unconventional roles. As a child, I revered this part of my mother: the young woman in long braided hair who dared to speak for women in a country ruled by men. Mama disguised her role as a female soldier in training. She hid her military uniform in her school bag from her teachers and told her family that she was staying after school at a friend's house.

"I did that for weeks," she said, until the war was over.

Mama shared the army's will to claim a land she had never visited. Her national identity as a Pakistani was linked intricately to Kashmir, a remote valley that my mother had learned about in childhood from her mother's stories. "I am from Kashmir," she said, but shied away from saying "I am a Kashmiri." Mama held on to Kashmir as if it were a timeless picture in a vintage frame. She had romanticized the valley. It is *Jannat*, or Paradise, a term coined by the late Mughal emperor Jahangir. He wrote, "If there is paradise on earth, it is here, it is here, it is here in Kashmir." For Mama, the valley had old-world charm. She saw it through iconic photographs: sun-kissed images of *shikaras*, small canoes, gliding along Dal Lake; blue-green mountains; and worshippers at sacred places bobbing their heads like sparrows.

From Mama's hometown in Lahore, Pakistan-held Kashmir is at least a six-hour car ride—a drive she's never taken.

After the 1965 war, Mama became a loyalist for the newly created Pakistan People's Party, led by the socialist Zulfikar Ali Bhutto, whom my mother worshipped. "When I saw this handsome man speak, I was hooked. I made my decision to help him win the election," she said.

Mama went door to door with her one-line slogan: "Let your women vote." She told me, "I wanted our women to come out of their homes. I had to convince the men that the women had a right to vote . . . everything in Pakistan begins with men. They control the country, and men often control the lives of women."

On December 7, 1970, Bhutto won by a landslide. It was a historic day for the country. Many years later, memories of the 1970 election lie in a faded black-and-white photograph of my mother on the front page of the *Imroz* ("Today") newspaper, which is no longer published. In the picture, Mama sports a white cotton shirt and baggy pants, her long hair braided. With one hand in the air, clenched in a fist, she looks like a fighter. She has the aura of a young woman on the verge of achieving her dreams.

She was my first woman warrior.

As her daughter, I'm often amazed at how *unwounded* my mother is. She would readily admit that war changes everything and everyone. It changed the ways in which women behaved: how they planned their day and how they interacted with one another, and carefully choosing how they communicated with outsiders. War could leave deep wounds that would never heal, but somehow it didn't mark my mother, or at least there were no visible injuries. Her only melancholic moments come when remembering her mother. "She sacrificed so much. For most of her life, she was alone and bitter, always wanting more than her country could give her."

I remember my grandmother, whom I affectionately called Nano, as a woman with a sickness, nausea, and longing that I had at times felt when I looked at the past. We spent nights together in Lahore. In her nineties, she had long, thin gray hair; steel-gray eyes; and hands that felt like leather. She slept with dangling gold and emerald earrings, and as she aged, her voice cracked when she spoke. She lived alone in the old quarter of Krishnagar. Nano's house once belonged to a Hindu family before Pakistan was a country. In the late 1940s, the family migrated to India when it became an independent state. Even after the freedom movement, the neighborhood retained its Hindu name—Krishna is a revered god in Hinduism.

Though Pakistan became her home, Nano's family was once rooted in Kashmir before the valley and the entire Indian subcontinent became unevenly split by the Partition Plan, drafted by Britain's Sir Cyril Radcliffe, who had never set foot in the region.[1] In five weeks, the Radcliffe Line, or the border formally recognized by England and Indian nationalists, divided millions of Christians, Hindus, Muslims, and Sikhs. When the British government withdrew, it transferred power from all of its 584 princely states to the newly created countries of India and Pakistan.

All except Kashmir.

Nano's house generated many stories: The story of moving into a space previously owned by Hindus before India and Pakistan declared their independence. The story of everyone living together, even after marriage, as one big family. And the story of grandchildren playing on the flat rooftop of the house while Nano, their caretaker, watched with joy. For decades, the house was the center of Nano's life, complete with history and family fables. As her family structure changed, when children and grandchildren moved out, the house she once cherished for the infectious love it contained rearranged itself into empty spaces. All that was left were memories of a time and place retold as fragments of her imagination. "We had apple trees in Kashmir," she would say of a place she could never forget.

During my visits to Pakistan, I spent a few nights with Nano. Most of my days were spent traveling through Pakistan to interview and research victims of violence, speak to scholars about terrorism trends, and meet with government officials to understand the rising terrorist threat in the country. Over a span of thirty years, the Pakistan I came to know was unfamiliar and unrelated to Mama's experiences as a child and a young adult. After my parents purchased their first and only home in Texas, Mama made it clear that she could never return to a country obsessed with its own survival from political chaos, corruption, crime, and calculated terrorist attacks. "Who can live in a place where random violence is the norm?" she lamented.

The stories of a distant time and Mama's training as a soldier that I had heard as a child forced me to question the role of women in war. I had to know more about what motivated a woman to fight for a cause she believed in. In my mind, I came up with questions I might someday ask women living in or exposed to conflict: Have you ever come into contact with cases of family violence or experienced violence yourself? Have you been a victim of a traumatic incident? How do you perceive conflicts in the Muslim world? What is your practice of Islam? And so on. Behind such clumsy questions was an impatient attempt to get to the most direct question of all: Who are you?

At the heart of these questions was an attempt to piece together the identity of Muslim girls and women in order to understand their experiences and choices. As a young Muslim girl in America, I carried the burden of adapting to a mainstream society while belonging to a distinct and decidedly fixed culture at home. Although I was not raised in conflict or exposed to a constant stream of violent action, I had a different conflict, which has been described as a clash of cultures. I wrote poetry to heal, expressing the realities and dangers of an honor-and-shame culture that could entrap a Muslim girl in a Western country, if she was exposed, over time, to severe adverse life events, such as trauma, childhood victimization, neglect, abuse, depression, anxiety, or family instability. I firmly believed in the principle that a person is the product of his or her environment. Thus, I felt, Muslim girls and women made different choices depending on where they were in life. Often, it seemed, these choices were driven by a belief in dreams and the hopeless illusion that Islam would prevail with violent action.

The more I learned, the more I understood how conflicts could drive some women and girls to take up arms and sacrifice everything for the greater good, which is *one* part in the ongoing story of females looking to belong to a cause, country, or creed. When I became a young adult, I learned about the power and ubiquitousness of stories. My longtime professor friend Eric Selbin said of revolutionary stories, "Memories of oppression, sagas of occupation and struggle, tales of opposition, myths of once and future glory, words of mystery and symbolism, are appropriated from the pantheon of the history of resistance and rebellion common to almost every culture . . . and provide a picture of the world as it was, as it is, and as it could and should be."

I see Mama, now in her sixties, in her revolutionary imagination, wondering what life might have been, had she stayed in Pakistan instead of coming to America as a young wife with me in her arms.

"I could have been a great politician," she said.

In seventh-century Arabia, the Archangel Gabriel revealed God's message to the Prophet Muhammad. Believers in Islam, the world's fastest-growing religion, with over a billion Muslims and a rising rate of conversion, see the life-altering gift of faith as their guide in this world and their path to Paradise, which is the ultimate goal. Muslims learn about the human condition from past prophets and saintly men and women, whose stories are preserved and transmitted by historians, intellectuals, and deeply thoughtful students who understand the past with passionate hearts.

At home, religion was described to me as an event in history. Islam was something that happened—a moment of truth that came to be, which was both singular and magical but existed in a fixed time period. Daddy constantly criticized Muslims for their backwardness, corruption, and religious rioting. He condemned faith-based rituals and lived by a stubborn logic he called the *cause-and-effect* principle, which meant that faith alone was not the answer to ignorance and inexperience. Faith could not save us from ourselves.

Mama disagreed. She believed in the Promised Land and rarely let life discourage her. Her abiding faith in God reminded me of the Christian preacher Joel Olsteen, who said, "You may face problems and setbacks, but remember, God is still leading the way." My mother's approach was relaxed and confident. She made faith both accessible and ultramodern, allowing me to discover it for myself later in life. I've always thought that was one of the beauties in her practice—she lifted the pressures over hijab and sexuality and allowed her daughters to come into their own. "Because you are a Muslim girl, you have to be strong," she said repeatedly.

Mama taught me to memorize a few verses in Arabic from the holy book, the Quran, and recited a popular oral tradition: "Paradise lies at the feet of mothers." Early on, I knew I couldn't talk back to the woman who determined if I entered Heaven or Hell.

As a child, I had mixed images of Mama. I watched her dance with her Indian and American friends in our home. Daddy turned our home into a disco. Photographs show a strobe light hanging from the ceiling of the living room. With the furniture shoved aside, men and women of different faiths and ethnic background twirled to the music. Some drank. In her red dress, Mama danced the night away sober.

As an immigrant child, I was confused about many things, among them the role of religion in family, society, and the larger world. While I didn't learn the history, doctrine, or principles of Islam at home, my parents did teach me the fundamentals of success: be kind to everyone, show up on time, and work hard. However, I needed to know more about Islam and believed in the spiritual depth of rituals and the circle of life, as described by Joseph Campbell in *The Power of Myth*: "The circle represents totality. Everything within the circle is one thing, which is encircled, enframed. That would be the spatial aspect. But the temporal aspect of the circle is that you leave, go somewhere, and always come back. God is the alpha and the omega, the source and the end. The circle suggests immediately a completed totality, whether in time or in space."[2] Though Campbell wrote about mythology and the hero's journey, his concept that "the whole world is a circle" helped me embrace the "circle of faith" idea.

In my lectures, I say that Muslims believe that Islam completes the circle of all monotheistic religions, and therefore Islam is not a new but a "borrowed" religion, building on the tenets of Judaism and Christianity, led by a prophet from Arabia sent by God to remind people of His Oneness and His Greatness. In that spirit, a

Muslim is "one who submits" to the will of God; and in submission, or worship of the one God, a Muslim enters the Afterlife. (Oddly, the goal for pious, practicing Muslims is the same for Muslim extremists, who use violence and any means necessary to attain a place in Paradise.)

Everything about faith baffled and stirred me. As a child, I had more than Islam to inform my understanding of faith. I learned from Jewish teachers, a Methodist preacher, Southern Baptists, Sufi mystics, and Catholic friends. I watched my father's Hindu friends worship their deities at holy festivals. I heard the names of Lord Krishna and Ganesh, the elephant god, at dinner parties. With school friends, I attended church and listened to calls of "Hallelujah" and high-pitched voices rising to the altar; I heard the faithful pray to the Son and invoke the Trinity. I learned about the simplicity and straightforwardness of Zen Buddhism in class and how to find enlightenment in something as simple and profound as a bowl of rice. At private parties, I watched long-bearded men from Afghanistan spin in circles, their Sufi hearts flamed with the love of God.

With the confidence of youth, I had the unshakable belief that God is Great and He created humans to emulate His attributes: mercy, patience, gratitude, and compassion. No matter what or how much I learned about religion, I realized that God is, in the words of novelist Yann Martel, "as God should be. With shine and power and might. Such as can rescue and save and put down evil."[3] To believers of God, He is *enough*. Which I only accepted after years of studying (and partly experiencing the effects of) violence, trauma, and the psychology of evil; and only after I found beauty in the wisdom and love of God from self-aware, placid Muslims, a reminder from the Quran that "believers are each other's mirrors." Self-awareness, however, is only a lantern in the courtyard of a house that will go dark within hours, days, or months. I needed a spiritual teacher for life to find enlightenment.

Those early years proved that I didn't know the mysteries of Islam: the meaning of the face veil, segregated spaces, and the immense power of men over women in almost every aspect of their lives. Threading myself through the experiences of women in distant places, as well as behind closed doors in America, I learned of families entangled in their hidden traumas; of women hunted like animals in the wilderness for so-called honor crimes; of the weight of clerical decisions clamped on fragile, voiceless girls; and of women choosing violence, even when not directly experiencing it, because it made sense to them. While I could not possibly understand all that afflicts women, I wanted to map the psychological, physical, and personal histories of women who conformed to the vertical lines of violent behavior.

In contrast with violent women, between the stories of war told by my mother and the questions of faith narrated by my father, lies a world of women who are strong and immutable. The righteous Muslim woman is proud of the rights granted to her in seventh-century Arabia, Islam's glorious past. Today, the same rights and privileges of Muslim women are dictated by a patriarchy of irrational and ignorant men, many of whom support the radical interpretation of Islam—the barbarism, the beastly action, and a culture of humiliation and shame narrated by violent extremists. These same men prey on vulnerable women, who are misguided, misinformed, and mistaken, incapable of differentiating the universal values of love that the Quran promotes from the teachings of corrupt, crooked men with blood on their hands. To uncover the illusions of violent women, I would have to *know* them, or at least try to trace the depth, or the shallowness, of their actions.

And so I did, or at least I tried, like so many terrorism analysts and scholars around the globe, surrendering their working hours to the complex world of extremism. We entered the dark, dense study of evil that crushes the voice of reason, and I, the first Muslim woman in the Counterterrorism Center, found this work at times suffocating, wanting to let in air when the fear of drowning in the stories of women committing unspeakable, unthinkable crimes swirled in night dreams.

Through the stories of violent women, I turned to Islam's rich history and cultural traditions to better understand the role of violence and, by extension, suicide. I found answers in the Quran and the hadith literature. I learned a glaring truth: No Muslim woman or man has the right to choose death over life. Muslims believe that dying is proscribed by God and is not a destined choice. The Quran and numerous sayings by the Prophet ban suicide. If religion is unambiguous on prohibitions against suicide and suicide terrorism, then why do women choose to die? How can women justify a sin so clearly forbidden by the Prophet? Muhammad said, "The gates of Heaven are forever closed to anyone who takes his [or her] own life." Only God has the right to choose a person's time of death.

The ban on suicide is clear, as is the prohibition on extremism and extremist behavior. Islamic scripture emphasizes the "middle way" and not "overstepping the bounds" ordained by God. Muslims are taught to live a balanced life and avoid extremes because to do otherwise contradicts God's law. "Do not exceed the bounds in your religion" is a popularly cited verse in the Quran, along with numerous sayings in the oral tradition such as "Beware of extremism in your religion."

In Islamic history, the first extremists were a group called the *Khawarij*; they murdered the Prophet's son-in-law, Ali, in a town in Iraq and killed both of Ali's sons, who were also the Prophet's grandsons. In her book, *Islam: A Short History*, religious scholar Karen Armstrong wrote of the *fitna*, or "chaos," in the early Islamic period in which Muslims killed each other for power, greed, revenge, and religious supremacy.[4] The wars that began so long ago in Islamic history are being fought today by a new brand of extremists, and women are among them.

Embedded in my research are "master narratives," which are the study of what narratives "do": how extremists use stories and narratives of violent extremism to recruit new members, strengthen their base, and motivate actions. In *Master Narratives of Islamist Extremism*, one of the authors writes that stories and narratives "reveal a great deal about how members of such extremist groups think about where they came from and where they might be going, how they should be organized, what goals they should pursue in light of what they believe, and what makes them (as 'true' followers of the Prophet Muhammad) unique."[5] Unlike men, extremist women may find alternative meaning in war stories and usually respond with a different sense of personal purpose that connects them to the community and the historical imagination of the Islamic cosmos. It's not surprising that women crystallize their intentions, needs, and desires apart from men, even in the trappings of war.

Above all, I have learned that the motives of women are *personal*, which is now supported by research but was, at the time, a hunch that fluttered into my work. That terrorism could be personal was more than a prediction or a premonition. I had my own research notes and a tapestry of interviews that read like a short-story collection rife with descriptions and details I wished I had not known, even though each tale was powerful and electrifying. I came to witness truths that were larger and more meaningful than the literature on terrorism would allow—among them, that female terrorists believed they were being authentic by choosing violent action. The existing literature of female terrorism and the reasons attached to why women kill reads like a fantastical novel, which explains why the subject of female terrorists is often perceived as opaque and illusory by authorities and intelligence agencies. In my experience, it is only when a woman perpetrates a deadly attack that authorities take action and begin to ask the same questions: Why now? Who is she? And how can we minimize the threat?

Over the years, I've heard conflicting explanations of why women join extremist groups. Some terrorism analysts argue that these women are desperate: they have no choice but to die. Others consider a woman's psychological condition: she is labeled insane, mentally ill, traumatized, or terrified. Many argue that violence in women is unnatural, a capability that could only be taught by maniacal men. In my own lectures, I point to the powerful concepts of honor and shame: women choose suicide terrorism to honor their broken lives, to discard the shame of their sins in *this* life to restore honor in *that* life; these women may believe that suicide terrorism is the only way into Heaven. For women in love with a terrorist, peace comes in martyrdom.

No research study of violent women, or men or children, has offered a comprehensive "root causes" explanation to help us understand violent behavior. In nearly twenty years of studying this phenomenon, I've found that empirical evidence of violent behavior is often representative of a specific time, place, culture, and woman. There are no universal truths, only patterns. Over the years, the models shaped by terrorism experts to underscore the dangers of extremism and the various variables that explain violence may have been overemphasized. For example, underlying social and economic grievances could be possible motives for *one* woman, which is why there are no single or simple coherent narratives. There are numerous narratives, and the dialect of survival for each woman—a story that is her own—has to be considered in the absence of empirical evidence.

Today, radical women present a real and ongoing threat. Discovering who they are is the first step to understanding the allure of extremism. Because of my mother's role in fighting for Kashmir, it seemed logical to begin my journey in the bowl-shaped valley to meet the bomb girl.

Chapter Two

# GOING SOLO

## *Indian-held Kashmir*

A flock of birds circled above like paper butterflies. The smell of the place was a combination of wood, apples, and morning rain. The young woman I called Sadia led the protest with one arm swinging through the air, her voice loud and brassy like the sound of a solo trumpet. "We want freedom!" she shouted. The women looked like an undefeated army; their chants filled the tepid air. In sharp tones, they chanted: "What do we want? *Azaadi!* What do we need? *Azaadi!* What are we fighting for? We want freedom! Kashmir belongs to us!"

I closed my eyes and felt their thundering voices. Their desire for freedom was reasonable. The women needed to be heard by the battalion of Indian police waving their batons. In their togetherness, the women displayed a solidarity that was intuitively felt: *They had been destined for one another.* With each street protest, they closely held on to a feeling of necessity and the uniqueness of their actions. When I opened my eyes, I locked gazes with Sadia, whose eyes squinted as though she was smiling at me from behind the cloth that covered her face. Something about her made me want to comfort her, offer her reassurance, a hand to hold—to say, "You are free. No one can take away your conscience."

I leaned to the side of a brick wall in a short teal shirt and matching scarf falling loosely over my head. Under a saffron sun, I watched an elderly woman in a white dress squat on the ground. Her face looked worn. She held a large white poster lettered in red: "United Nations, where are you?" It was an indication of the betrayal by the international community, like a lover who had proved unfaithful. Kashmiris expected India and Pakistan to hold the plebiscite they had agreed to in 1948 at the United Nations. They expected to decide their political future. But the vote never transpired.

The women's discordant voices and jarring movements felt familiar. These women could have been in any part of the Muslim world. This could have been Algeria, Egypt, Iraq, Pakistan, or any number of Western countries where women used the streets to grab the world's attention. One salient feature about Muslim women today is that they are increasingly active in political and violent movements. Like their men, they demand the right to be heard.

"Protests are the only way out for people to vent their anger," one Kashmiri woman said.

In Kashmir, women protest when their children disappear or die from torture. Like their men, they rebel against what they call an Indian occupation. They use the streets to share their stories of the defeated. The women of Kashmir march to send a broader social message. "Women defend women," one activist said. In 2004, on International Human Rights Day, the women of Srinagar swarmed the streets to oppose the rape of Shabnam Bano, a twelve-year-old girl, by an Indian Army major in Handwara. The women wailed as they held up a photograph of the girl. On the front page of a local newspaper, an Indian female police officer is shown tearing the girl's picture. That clipping forced me to imagine what I might have done if I had been raised in *that* culture. Would I join the women screaming rage and resentment toward the army? Or would I shoulder a heavy silence and live in a globe of darkness, ignoring the traumas and threats around me? It's difficult for an outside observer to accept that in a protracted conflict, women and girls have limited opportunities—their lives are continually interrupted by gunfire, shelling, curfews, shutdowns, and protests. And so it is understandable that with few or no options to express themselves, women and girls find the streets to be an ideal setting for their sailing voices.

The female protesters fearlessly moved forward. I followed them, observing them from a distance. I was a witness to an event that happened over and over across the valley. The women exclaimed in Urdu, a language that the Indian security forces understood. The leader of the procession held a small sports-type megaphone. I heard her thundering voice.

Kashmir is a valley with nearly eighty-six thousand square miles set between blue-white mountains, rolling forested hills, shimmering lakes, and endless farms. A fraction of the world's population lives in Kashmir. More than ten million in Jammu and Kashmir reside in India, which is two million more than the number of people in Virginia, where I live. Nearly six million Kashmiris live in the autonomous territory of Pakistan. The Chinese regions of Aksai Chin and Trans-Karakoram Tract account for 19 percent of Kashmir, an area the size of Maryland, disputed by India. Its highest peak is the Siachen Glacier, where Indian and Pakistani troops engage in tit-for-tat border clashes like schoolyard bullies. Kashmir is the world's highest battlefield; India and Pakistan have waged war over Kashmir.

In the backdrop of Kashmir are almost a million soldiers, rifles at their shoulders, without a trace of bravura in their eyes. In winter, royal-blue snowflakes fall like ice jewels. In summer, Indian-held Kashmir is a green candy bowl bursting with color. The smell of wood and clay hangs in the air. When I first arrived, Srinagar felt like an amusement park. Tourists glided along Dal Lake in shikaras, weaving their way through a floating vegetable garden and a patch of pale-pink water lilies. Children ran up and down the majestic stairs to the entrance of the Mughal garden lined with plum-purple peonies and wild roses. Local boys swam in the lake with the sun on their backs.

That summer day, I listened to the words reverberating through the air like an ancient song. Sadia spoke, and her followers repeated her words, their raucous voices louder than microphones could project. Alongside her was Yasmine Raja, the head of Muslim Khawateen Markaz (Muslim Women's Organization), or MKM, who was once beaten so badly in jail that she limps on one leg. Being part of the MKM gave young women like Sadia a sense of purpose and belonging. I suspected that the women's group gave her the cover she needed. Men found her do-or-die attitude endearing, and they saw her as graceful and genuine. But to an outsider like myself, Sadia was dangerously spirited and self-serving.

The women moved together at a snail's pace. Their voices were too loud, too shrill. They wanted to reach Lal Chowk, the center of the city. "They will never make it," a male activist said. He stood near me for my protection. "They will be arrested right here." Under the 1958 Armed Forces Special Powers Act (AFSPA), anyone in Kashmir can be detained for any reason. Under the terms of the law, Indian authorities have unrestricted powers. Kashmiri novelist Mirza Waheed elaborated on India's catch-and-kill policy: "My friends, *all* my friends, went away too, and God only knows if they will ever come back. Not many do, you see, and those who do, don't live very long here. Because the army has decided there is only one way of dealing with the boys: catch and kill. *Catch and kill.*"[1]

Police jeeps blocked the road. They were surrounded by a swarm of journalists and photographers. They snapped and clicked. Guards posed for pictures. It was an all-too-familiar scene for the authorities. No one was worried. Female guards pushed the protesters back with batons the size of a baseball bat. The women stopped. They continued shouting. They were unafraid of jail. I had learned that authorities used temporary arrest to break the momentum, but the women I knew in Kashmir were unmoved.

Standing next to me, former militant leader Farooq Ahmed Dar boasted, "Our women are strong. The Indians think they can humiliate them by throwing them in jail. But when they are released, they will protest again," he said. Dar believed that Kashmiri women could tolerate extreme hardship. These women had an instinct for survival. Dar, who towered over me, stood near me like a bodyguard. He was in his forties, broad-shouldered with smashing brown eyes, a Roman nose, and dark hair brushed aside. Dar and I observed the protesters from the sidelines, standing against a brick wall of an old, empty building, watching the women move slowly toward the police. Someone yelled *"Allahu Akbar!"* ("God is great!") into the microphone, followed by one long cheer. Cameras zoomed.

"Our women are no different than men," Dar told me.

We moved closer to the brick wall. Shabir, an ex-militant and a member of Dar's organization, said to me, "These women share our goals. They have our aspirations. They are fighters like us. They are ready to die for a cause." The belief in a better life after death is a central tenet of the Islamic faith, which explains why protesters are unafraid. Men admire women for being tireless champions of the independence movement.

At a comfortable distance, I watched female police officers shove Sadia and Yasmine Raja into the back of a jeep. Journalists poked their cameras into their faces. *Click! Click! Click!* The men watched their women being taken away. It was a chilling sight.

"This is another day in Kashmir," Dar said.

I assumed that the women would be released in days. That someone would take them home, perhaps a family friend or relative. As protesters, they hadn't committed a crime. They didn't present a security threat. They hadn't used violence, carried weapons, issued threats, or used abusive language. Before I could ask, Dar gave me an answer. "The police will release them the next day. They know they can't keep these women. They just spend a night or two in jail. It's nothing to worry about," he said, half-smiling.

On the dusty road, women began to disperse. Slowly, they put down their signs and moved in different directions, their faces like wounded instruments. "They will try again," someone said. "Our women never stop trying."

Even as the crowd dispersed, a middle-aged woman stood facing the warm glow of the sun and chanted softly, her body swaying. "What do we want? What do we need? *Azaadi!*" The sun beat brightly on her black robe. "We will return," she said in an ethereal voice.

However, being a protester was not enough for Sadia. "If I cannot live, then I want to die," she told me before her arrest. She believed in martyrdom and everything it stood for. To die in a suicide mission would give her the chance to live again. She wanted to go to a better place and live in the *other* world.

There was nothing unusual about Sadia, except for her beautiful pearl-gray eyes and milky skin. Like other Kashmiri girls I met, she was committed to change the conflict and unmistakably made the wrong choice when she desired death. Her decision to die violently was a choice that most Kashmiri women do not make. *Violence blurs time, present and future,* I thought. *Violence will not change the conflict.*

For a brief period, she was my young guide. One July morning, as flies buzzed lazily and soldiers gawked when we walked by, Sadia shared her well-kept secret.

"I volunteered for a suicide mission," she said casually. "The men turned me away. They said, 'We don't need women.' But they are wrong. They need *me.*"

It was the most unforgettable walk I had taken with anyone. For a moment, I could not see her strapped to a bomb, ready to pull the trigger to end her life. But I knew, from speaking to other women in other places, that the wish of the martyr is profound: she wanted to fly to Heaven.

*Doesn't Islam forbid this?* I wanted to shake Sadia. I knew Islam better than this young woman raised in a conservative Muslim culture.

I tried to understand what could cause an attractive, intelligent young woman like Sadia to choose death over life. She didn't look like a hardened criminal or terrorist. At first glance, she didn't appear emotionally unstable or mentally ill. But I knew that violent women don't fit any profile. A female bomber can be young or old, single or married, widowed, a mother. With more than a decade of research, the academic and intelligence communities have yet to agree on whether psychological profiles of extremist women are a useful way to understand their drive to commit violent acts. What we do know is that common themes exist, largely reflected by personal grievances, which include perceived injustice and the indiscriminate use of violence by authorities on distressed Muslim communities and individuals.

What all these women have in common is their commitment to a cause. For Sadia, the freedom of Kashmir from Indian occupation was the only reason that mattered, that was worth dying for. But luckily for her, the Pakistan-based extremist group she wanted to join, Lashkar-e-Taiba, or LeT, wanted nothing to do with her—at least not at that time.

Still, I wondered. Was I overlooking something? What explained Sadia's motives? Was she abused as a child? Did someone hurt her? Did she lose someone in her family? Did she witness unthinkable acts of aggression? Did she want to prove to men that she was capable? What did her family say about all this? Did they know? There were too many unanswered questions. The only answer I did have was that Sadia had the common emotions of a would-be martyr: she was determined, distressed, angry, and likely wounded by what she had witnessed growing up in conflict.

As a result of the ongoing crisis, countless women I have interviewed in the valley have exhibited signs of anxiety, depression, and trauma. They don't sleep. Some have nightmares. They can't eat. One woman lost her voice when she found out that her youngest son had been thrown in jail for a crime she says he didn't commit. Many women take drugs, antidepressants to cope with conflict. Others, like Sadia, seek comfort and strength in a movement. They are part of something larger than themselves and wish to forget their individual grievances. Being part of a movement creates a sense of belonging and offers women a wider community, other than their immediate family members.

As noon approached, the breeze stopped. I followed Sadia to a shady spot. We stood near each other, leaning against a brick wall. In that moment, I cried in silence. I tried to avoid her luminous eyes and imagined myself climbing mountains, if only to forget this girl with an idealized vision of herself as a suicide bomber.

"The men didn't have to refuse me," she said.

*You have so much to live for. You can continue studying. Stay single or get married. Have children if you wish. You do not know what you are saying. Why is death the solution to your problems? Do you really think you will find Paradise after you detonate? What could you possibly gain by wishing for martyrdom?* These thoughts filled me with contempt when I should have shown sympathy. As an American Muslim woman, no matter how grave the situation, I could not forget or forgive a suicide bomber. Even though I believed in the power of mercy and the triumph of love and hope, I could see that Sadia had failed, or someone failed her during childhood or in her young adult life. Somewhere in her background, the details of which were hidden from me, there was cowardice, weakness, laziness, dishonesty, stupidity, and a void that comes from an unsatisfied existence.

"I quit the organization."

Sadia was referring to the LeT. In November 2008, the group perpetrated one of the deadliest terror attacks ever, across India's financial hub, Mumbai. The reign of terror killed more than 150 Indians. Founded by Hafiz Saeed, for whose capture there is a $10 million reward in the United States, the LeT is arguably Pakistan's prized weapon against the mighty Indian Army. Pakistan continues to publicly deny ideological, logistical, and financial support for LeT, a point still debated. Thankfully, India restrained itself and did not go to war with Pakistan but agreed to a joint investigation. The Kashmir peace process perished. In 2013, clashes along the guarded border further disrupted any effort to press for a political solution in Kashmir.

"I had no choice," Sadia said, her eyes on the black gate ahead of us. "I joined a women's organization. Women do two things: they stay at home or protest. But we need something more."

She leaned toward me. "I have to find a way to convince other girls like me that jihad is the only way," she whispered. Suddenly, I witnessed an innocent-looking girl turn to violence for a false sense of security. Sadia forced me to imagine looking through her eyes. *What can I do to prove that there is an alternative to violence?* I thought. *Is it possible for me to simply say that "life is beautiful" when her life is marked by anger and rage—the by-products of trauma—and brutal, shocking acts committed by both the military and militants?*

The would-be bomb girl helped me accept that her world was turned upside-down. In a way, Sadia was not wrong to want to *do* something meaningful with her life and awaken the world community to the never-ending war in Kashmir. She was not wrong to seek happiness and imagine her prized home lifted from occupation. Her greatest weakness was in believing that violence was the answer. There was something of a paradox in my brief relationship with Sadia: I could understand how she might choose violence, though I find it difficult to empathize with anyone, regardless of faith, who destroys human life.

By now, I had grown tired of Kashmir's secrets. In a conflict like this, almost everyone sheltered a secret from the authorities. A mother would protect her son from arrest and lie about where he was hiding. A wife would pretend that she didn't know her husband was a militant. A daughter could forgive her mother for deciding to lead a movement, therefore making less time for her, and never fully understand it.

On the dusty road, it was impossible to know if Sadia could be callous, careless, or crazy. She had known me for a few hours and somehow believed she could trust me. I suspect that she wanted someone from the outside to listen and understand her. Sometimes, all a person needs is a stranger to show sympathy.

I watched Indian guards pace up and down the street, twirling thick wooden sticks, their primary weapon.

Sadia stopped and raised her head to the sky. Falcons circled above the trees. We heard their cries.

She continued, "When I was eighteen years old, I was a member of Lashkar. I was convinced that I could be successful. We were planning a major attack. But the operation was put on hold. I don't know what happened next. The brothers told me that there were enough men; they didn't need a woman to attack India. I did not expect this.

"The men were foolish," she said in a passionate display of defiance. "I have a responsibility to my people. Do you understand?"

I nodded in disbelief. *And who would be responsible for your actions?* Sadia may have sounded determined, but she was confused. Her abstract picture of a holy war that would alter the political landscape of Kashmir was a fantasia. I assumed that she experienced flashes of glory, moments when she could imagine herself a martyr.

"The men don't see my power. They don't think I can do it."

Strap on the bomb? She made it sound like putting on a lace dress. Her unbridled spirit was enviable and dangerous.

As we kept walking, the sun's warm gold light danced on the rooftops of houses we passed. In a small garden nearby, flowers resembled luxurious wrapping paper.

"The world will know what is going on here if I do this. No one sees Kashmir."

"That's not true."

"It's the only way."

"They do see you. I talk about Kashmir all the time. I teach. I write. Some Americans do care," I protested. I thought of lectures I had given and articles I had written on Kashmir, starting with one in the Summer 2008 issue of *Ms.* magazine titled "Kashmiri Women Speak Out," with Sarah Wachter. Stories of Kashmir appeared infrequently in the Western press, which is why Kashmir, to most Westerners, is an invisible conflict.

"I want to be a martyr," Sadia said again.

*This can't be the way to Paradise,* I thought. *Martyrdom means "to bear witness" and to sacrifice in God's name. Only self-defense is allowed in Islam. Never violence for the sake of violence.* I remembered an oral tradition by the Prophet of Islam that rejected suicide: "The gates of Heaven will be closed forever to anyone who takes his [or her] own life." Maybe Sadia didn't want to accept the tradition, or she had mental health problems I was unaware of. There was so much about her that I didn't know.

Luckily, Kashmir did not have a history of female suicide bombers. There was only one report. In October 2005, a twenty-two-year-old Kashmiri woman named Hafsa blew herself up minutes before an Indian Army convoy passed along a highway in Awantipora, a town twenty miles south of Srinagar.[2] Very little was known about her. According to Kashmiri journalist Basharat Peer, his investigation claimed that she had had an affair with a militant and ran home to join him. His study suggested that "there are social taboos against girls willingly marrying Pakistani militants, and if they do, they are no longer acceptable to the conservative Kashmiri society."[3] The female bomber was a member of the Daughters of Ayesha, a women's wing of Jaish-e-Muhammad, another radical group based in Pakistan.

Sadia and I walked toward the chinar tree. The mountains in the distance curved down like galaxies over green rolling hills. I stole glances at the would-be martyr. I wanted to know why she was different. During my trips to the valley, no girl or woman I had met had aspirations to be a suicide bomber, so why now? Had this young woman chosen violence, or had violence chosen her?

Trying to understand motivations of a would-be suicide bomber is almost impossible. Most terrorism scholars make calculated guesses based on too few factors. In *Women, Gender, and Terrorism*, I tried to offer an explanation: "The reasons why women participate in violence will vary, even where common grievances are present, but what motivates women to engage in suicide terrorism is bound to be different for each *individual* woman."[4] I still believe the study of gender-specific terrorism is limiting and based on too many generalizations to draw conclusions. If I wanted to stop Sadia, I had to get to know her.

At the time, all I could see was a beautiful young woman with a desire to act. She wanted something more than a college education and a married life. She wanted to change the conflict in Kashmir.

"You are a student," I said to her. "Your education will prove useful one day."

"I wish it were enough."

"God helps those in need."

"You can say this from America," she said with a hint of anger.

Sadia was right. I couldn't promise her a peaceful future when the Indian Army patrolled the streets and tracked everyone's movements like an intelligence agency. We were never alone.

I imagined Sadia to be the perfect recruit. Cloaked in a heavy black dress, she was unassuming and undetectable. She was less likely to be suspected and searched in a conservative outfit. In many Muslim cultures, women were prizes of men. Untouchables. Bloom argued that women with the will and capability to detonate "are the new stealth bomb."[5] Theirs is an unholy war.

When Sadia mentioned the word *jihad*, I began to think of what it meant in Islam. In an earlier essay, I had described jihad as an act of worship. It is a living, breathing concept.[6] *Jihad* originated in Arabic from the root words *ja ha da*, meaning to strive, to struggle, to seek goodness over evil. My father instilled in me his liberal, secular values, among them the belief that jihad is something private, not public, and the struggle for goodness is personal, not packaged with emotional responses to death.

Terrorists are clever to manipulate the meaning of jihad and avoid using the word *suicide*. They believe martyrdom operations to be legitimate, legal, and laudable. They have distorted the meaning of war and opt for suicide, their sacred act. It is the ultimate sacrifice, for which they expect a heavenly reward. Perhaps Sadia believed she could gain quick entry into Paradise with an explosives belt. She would not feel the pain of death. Her body would smell of musk. The only thing she couldn't do was wish for seventy-two male virgins. The concept of male and female virgin martyrs in Heaven is one of the most outlandish myths that extremists use for recruitment. The number seventy-two is not mentioned in the Quran, and the Arabic word *houri* is often mistaken for "virgin."

Sadia's drive to kill may have been personal. A respected friend, Dr. Jessica Stern of Harvard University, wrote that personal grievances "give rise to holy war."[7] Her list, which includes alienation, humiliation, and history, applies to protesters and political activists fighting the armed struggle in Kashmir.

Unfortunately, Sadia confused fighting for freedom with suicide operations. As an American Muslim woman, I had a responsibility to correct her. I needed to teach her "true" Islam.

"Suicide is forbidden. Besides, you're too young to die."

"Nothing happens when we protest. No one notices," Sadia said.

"You are doing something useful. You are a political activist. Violence isn't the solution in Kashmir. If you stay focused, one day Kashmir will be free. You have to trust God to guide you."

"I need help from the men. Talk to them. They like you," she told me.

*Are you listening to me? Why are you blinded by false notions of jihad? Don't you know that most Kashmiris are nonviolent? So why are you trying to be a rebel? Going solo is absurd.*

"How old are you?" I asked, changing the subject.

"Twenty-one."

"You can do so much." *Youth is a gift*, I thought.

"If you could see what I see, you would understand."

As we approached a black gate, she pleaded, "Talk to the men. They can help me."

The men she referred to were male political activists. At one time, they were gun-toting militants with anger toward their oppressors. Today, the same men are politicians, protesters, and participants in the conflict, a nonviolent resistance. They have reassured me that they can never return to terrorism. "We lost too many of our young men. They were arrested. Some disappeared. Some died fighting. Most died of torture," a senior ex-militant told me. He made it easy to understand why militants opted for a Gandhi-like approach. "Violence hurt us," he confirmed, referring to a long list of friends who died in the early 1990s.

Sadia and I pushed through the gate. A row of unassuming brown houses faced us; from one window, a group of women looked down at us. Sadia led me inside the house to meet the female activists.

"Please don't tell them," Sadia said. "They know nothing about this."

*What would I say to them? The bomb girl is waiting for an order?* Looking back, I have often wondered why Sadia chose to speak candidly to me. Maybe it's true that talking to a stranger can be less intimidating. Maybe Sadia believed that I had influence over the men. She knew they protected me. But I would say nothing to the men because I believed the call to martyrdom was a false promise—no freedom or justice would be served by Sadia's selfish surrender to suicide. Kashmir would remain as it had always been: forests untouched, inviting, dense, and green; a history of personal tragedies; and love and death passing as fragments of everyday life in a landscape of ruination.

A year later, I received a call from a senior leader. "She got married," he said. "Sadia moved to Mauritius with her husband."

"Thank God," I whispered. "She never strapped on the bomb."

Chapter Three

# DECEPTION

*Iraq*

The sound of his voice was heavy. In July 2014, the leader of the world's new terror nightmare, the Islamic State of Iraq and the Levant (ISIS), declared, "Rush, oh Muslims, to your state. Yes, it is your state. Rush, because Syria is not for the Syrians, and Iraq is not for the Iraqis. The Earth belongs to Allah!" Draped in black, Abu Bakr al-Baghdadi stood at the pulpit of the Great Mosque of al-Nuri in the Iraqi city of Mosul to separate the world into two: the believers (that is, the righteous followers of Islam) and the nonbelievers (or the *kufr*, which include "the camp of the Jews, the Crusaders, and their allies"). An old enemy disguised as new, al-Baghdadi made no mention of women. But his predecessor did.

The former al-Qaeda leader in Iraq, Abu Mus'ab al-Zarqawi, understood that Muslim women could inflict greater damage on his perceived enemies: the United States and its Muslim allies. Jordanian-born Al-Zarqawi reinvented the role of Muslim women by telling them to join the cause and be suicide bombers; marry an insurgent; recruit other women; and support terrorism by being a facilitator, messenger, logistics provider, and much more. Once jailed in Jordan, Al-Zarqawi was released in 1999 as part of a general amnesty granted by King Abdullah II but then sentenced to death a year after his release for the murder of a US diplomat. To Jordan and the rest of the world, Al-Zarqawi was a high-value target and a wanted man.

When Al-Zarqawi led al-Qaeda in Iraq, he encouraged women to join the movement. It's likely that Al-Zarqawi understood the unique role that female operatives could play, becoming effective weapons. He opened the space for women to join his dangerous organization to strap on the bomb and hit prime targets that men could not easily reach, such as tribal leaders, Shia mosques, the marketplace, police checkpoints, US coalition forces, and more. Perhaps Al-Zarqawi knew that women swaddled in layers of bulky clothing could breeze through public places and male-guarded checkpoints without being stopped; before the entry of female American soldiers, searching Muslim women in a conservative society was a cultural taboo.

I wasn't surprised. I knew from studying other conflicts that women take up arms when men call on them to join their revolutionary cause. For centuries, women, even my own mother, joined secular-nationalist movements to make a difference and effect change. Reading through the literature on women in war, I became convinced that Muslim female fighters are no different from secular women. They are often motivated by personal reasons, rather than political factors.

After leaving the Counterterrorism Center, I began to write and speak about women in the Islamic world. Al-Qaeda's war in Iraq enabled women to participate as equal partners in violence. In winter 2005, I published my first editorial piece, titled "The Bomber Behind the Veil," in the *Baltimore Sun* and predicted what I suspected to be true—female bombers would be the next stealth bomb: "An attack by a woman in one location could have a rippling effect and serve as a motivator for other women." Female attackers and accomplices surfaced in Afghanistan, Chechnya, Iraq, Israel, Pakistan, Uzbekistan, Jordan, and Western countries.

Al-Zarqawi may have been the first contemporary male terrorist leader to include female operatives, but he would not be the last. As a policy analyst at the Rand Corporation, I tracked the female terrorists of Iraq. When US troops entered Iraq in March 2003, a rare martyrdom video showed a forty-something Wadad Jamil Jassem declaring, "I have devoted myself to jihad for the sake of God and against the American, British, and Israeli infidels and to defend the soil of our precious and dear country." Jassem was not a member of al-Qaeda but proved early on that women could be deadly, determined, and decisive to the war, even when attacks by women appeared to be irregular and incidental acts of violence.

In 2005, two separate attacks by female operatives surprised authorities. On November 9, Muriel Degauque died in a suicide car bombing in Iraq. A Belgian convert to Islam, the thirty-eight-year-old Degauque intended to kill American troops, although she was the only one who died. Her attack marked the first time a Western woman had been successfully recruited for an operation in Iraq.

On the same day, an Iraqi woman whose brothers died fighting for al-Qaeda entered a wedding party in Amman, Jordan, to commit a deadly attack. Al-Qaeda sent a four-person team into Jordan from Iraq to target hotels frequented by Westerners, which included the Radisson, the Hyatt, and Days Inn. Sajida Al-Rishawi and her husband, Ali Hussein Ali al-Shamari, took cabs to the Radisson, wearing clothes fit for a wedding reception. Under her dress, Al-Rishawi had on an explosives belt with ball bearings, suggesting that she intended to inflict the largest number of casualties. Jordan's then–deputy prime minister, Marwan Muasher, told a press conference that the husband-and-wife hit team "entered the wedding hall. She pulled the detonator and it didn't go off. Her husband forced her to leave the hotel and then he blew himself up." The Radisson terrorist attack killed more than thirty civilians.

Al-Rishawi became the first Iraqi woman arrested for an unsuccessful bombing. Days later, she appeared on Jordanian state television and confessed to her crime. "In Jordan, we rented an apartment. [My husband] had two explosives belts. He put one on me and wore the other. He taught me how to use it, how to pull the cord and operate it," she said in Arabic. Al-Rishawi described the plan: how she would enter the hotel, moving to one corner while her husband went to another area.

She continued, "My husband executed the attack. I tried to detonate and it failed. I left. People started running and I started running with them." Later, Al-Rishawi retracted her confession and appealed her death sentence. Behind bars, she was forgotten until nearly ten years later, when ISIS demanded her release in exchange for Jordanian Air Force pilot Muath al-Kasasbeh, whom they had captured in Syria. The trade between the female operative and the pilot ended badly. When Jordan refused to swap Al-Rishawi, ISIS set the pilot on fire inside a steel cage. The barbaric act, which aired on television, horrified the Muslim and Western worlds. Beheadings, kidnappings, and ransom were common terrorist tactics, but burning a person alive was a gruesome and grisly act that had never been tried before. Al-Kasasbeh's burning led Jordan to execute Al-Rishawi by hanging on February 4, 2015.

The anomaly of female terrorists in Iraq confused security forces, including American authorities, because suicide attacks by women occurred randomly. In 2006, there were no attacks by women, even though male operatives continued to strike and kill American and Iraqi targets. Because attacks by women seemed rare—and were underreported and unprecedented—the world community didn't pay much attention to women in al-Qaeda.

But everything changed in 2007. In a lecture I gave at Columbia University, and later in Paris, I explained that male terrorists were increasing their efforts to recruit women to plan and perpetrate attacks. This move was both strategic and tactical—men could ensure the longevity of the terror organization by including women; and men could guarantee their own survival (i.e., avoid an arrest and death by authorities) when women were sent to strike the enemy targets. Bringing women into al-Qaeda helped the organization strike softer civilian targets as well as the predictable military targets. That year, there were at least six deadly attacks by women. In February, a woman detonated near a Shia college. Two months later, a female suicide bomber targeted police recruits, killing almost twenty officers. In the summer, a female bomber killed two policemen at a checkpoint. In the winter, a female attacker injured seven American soldiers near a military patrol; another attacker detonated near a police patrol, wounding five policemen; a female operative targeted the offices of a Sunni anti–al-Qaeda organization, killing fifteen people. All of the attacks took place in the Sunni triangle, an area in central Iraq near the capital city of Baghdad.

In 2008, the number of female bombers entered the double digits and included targets in the north, south, and west of Iraq. In most cases, there was little information about the identities and background of the female bomber and only more questions. Was she abused? Did someone force her? Was she raped or drugged? Who was her handler? With sketchy details of the female bombers, women became data points rather than human beings with a personal story that could explain why they had joined or been forced into violent extremism.

In 2008, three years after predicting the rise of female bombers, I published a piece in *Newsweek* titled "Dressed to Kill: Why the Number of Female Suicide Bombers Is Rising in Iraq."[1] Terrorism experts and security forces needed answers to explain the unusual upward trend. My explanation was simple: "As more men are captured or killed by security forces worldwide, it was inevitable that terror groups would consider other options to keep their cause alive." Violent men recognized that a Muslim woman has the ability to deceive, disguise, and destroy the enemy. Only a woman, in traditional or modern dress, can dupe men. She is capable of the greatest deception, using her gender to appear harmless and a victim of violence.

Many women are victims of the brutality of war, but in this case, women also became the victimizers, a term I borrowed from Dr. Mia Bloom, a terrorism scholar and friend. In a May 2007 article from eJournal USA, "Women as Victims and Victimizers," Bloom states that the ultimate goal of violent women is "to foster fear and uncertainty beyond the immediate victims by destroying lives and property in hopes of causing greater long-term costs."[2] Therefore, like men, women are capable of punishing or discriminating against another group, and killing is often the manner in which a female terrorist strikes at a sacrificial victim, which is exactly the definition of a victimizer. Bloom and I knew that women have a clear tactical advantage: by concealing their bombs under the long, loosely fitted *abaya*, women can blow themselves up almost anywhere. Therefore, the female bombers of Iraq fit the Three Cs framework. The local context and culture of Iraq at the time of war made it easy for women to join al-Qaeda and, later, ISIS. As bombers under the veil, women also proved to be highly capable, which gave extremist men a clear advantage.

In five years, Al-Zarqawi had managed to persuade a number of Muslim women to join him and al-Qaeda in Iraq (AQI). In his organization, females played a unique and never-before-seen role: to build a bomb, hide a bomb, or put one on. His primary goal had been to keep the men alive and ensure al-Qaeda's survival. For years, the use of female suicide terrorists ebbed and flowed, but the attacks and casualties that women inflicted on Iraq were enough to keep the world watching.

For US forces deployed in Iraq, the challenge of tracking female terrorists was enormous. A US Marine officer serving in Fallujah—a hotbed of extremist activity and sectarian strife—said to me, "If we are told by our superiors not to look at a woman because Arab culture tells us not to, then how are we supposed to suspect them?" Because women were seen as invisible non-state actors—they are independent of an established institution and act independently— the task of countering the threat of female terrorists was arguably greater than marginalizing al-Qaeda's men in Iraq. US authorities recognized that the anonymity of the female bomber protected her personal identity, making detection nearly impossible.

Not knowing the identities of female bombers in Iraq raised a number of security problems. If authorities do not know the names or faces of women who have committed attacks in Iraq and elsewhere, how can authorities counter the new threat? Is there a way to use deception to fight deception? The classic research question pulled me into the vast literature on deception as a common tactic used in warfare.

The *Shorter Oxford English Dictionary* defines the verb *deceive* as "to cause to believe what is false." The female bombers of Iraq mastered this skill. With a suicide belt hidden under their veils, women achieved two goals: they played into the stereotype steeped in Arab and Muslim culture that frames women as "the weaker sex" and victims of war, and they proved to be valuable operatives when they successfully exploded bombs hidden underneath their loose clothing. Therefore, men encouraged Muslim girls and women to join their group, setting a new cultural trend in motion and proving once again that culture trumps religion.

Since December 2007, attacks conducted by women have accounted for 36 percent, or five out of nineteen, of all suicide operations. During this time, I began to receive emails from US commanders in Iraq who were trying to understand the acts of violence by women and numerous calls by the media to explain the erratic behavior of al-Qaeda's women. A senior US Army officer involved with intelligence operations in Diyala, a restive province known for its orange trees, wrote to me in an email, "We have never viewed females with the same lethality as we would a male. And because of that cultural sensitivity on our part, it has made the female a very valuable tool of the insurgent." No doubt, Muslim cultural norms and tribal traditions protected women from becoming victims of violence. And often, men responded to war, not women, whom they viewed as their honor.

In an unclassified email from Iraq, US Army Major Garcia listed some observations about female suicide bombers. Given the difficult task of pinpointing specific characteristics of these people, the average demographics of known women involved in suicide operations for al-Qaeda in Iraq are generally as follows:

Younger females between the ages of eighteen and twenty-five.

Childless widows of AQI members who were martyred by ISF (international security forces) and want to exact revenge against the responsible organization.

Younger females who are not able to succeed in society or are maintained in an institution (mental hospital) without direct contact with family members.

> Young females who are brainwashed by
> daily AQI propaganda and a skewed interpretation
> of religious scriptures.

---

> Younger females with families (husband, children)
> who are coerced by AQI with compensation for
> their families.

---

According to this list, potential female recruits for al-Qaeda are young, widowed, or mentally ill. Suicide terrorism may have filled a void in their lives. But time has disproved the belief that *only* young females are attracted to male-dominated terrorist groups. In Iraq and in other conflicts, older women—married and with children—have joined violent groups. Age is not a predictable identifier for female terrorists.

If age does not matter, being a widow does. A US officer, who wished to be unidentified, told me of his experiences with widows who had bombs. "This weekend, we had two in Baquba [a city northeast of Baghdad in Diyala Province] . . . one [woman] wearing a vest that was stopped by a Son of Iraq when she was attempting to get into an area where a meeting was being held, which was followed five minutes later by another female driving a suicide car bomb less than four hundred meters away targeting first responders."

The stereotype of Muslim women as innocent and inactive participants of war changed the gender perception held by US soldiers and Iraqi forces that women could be female bombers. In 2008, the true-life stories of two different females—a child bomber and an older woman—showed that women could be more destructive than men. On average, they killed four times more people than male operatives. Women could have greater propaganda value when they shamed men and other women into joining al-Qaeda. And female bombers made for compelling news and international headlines because violence by women was a relatively new trend with varying conclusions.

In those early days, I told media outlets that women chose suicide terrorism for the same reasons as men. Many women expressed personal grievances against enemy forces; and family ties helped women enter terrorist organizations, a point that seemed obvious to me after looking at secular independence movements that often accepted female relatives of male leaders or operatives. *Why should the role of Muslim women be any different from that of other women?* I thought.

In a special feature for Al Jazeera English, I simplified the reason that women joined terror groups: Women used violence as a way to protest the breakdown of their social structures in war. Women protested the loss of their husbands, homes, and honor. Mothers felt the need to avenge the loss of their sons, for example. One Iraqi woman said, "There is no greater bond than a mother with her son. When her son is threatened, captured, or killed by security forces, then she has no reason to live. We take revenge by committing suicide attacks." Another said, "US troops destroyed my life, killed thousands of Iraqis, and have support from many who also are betrayers. I lost my children and husband, and have no reason to be in this world anymore."

Other women protested the devastating human rights conditions in Iraq since the 2003 war. In her book *City of Widows*, Iraqi journalist and activist Haifa Zangana wrote, "The Iraq war is a war against women."[3] An Iraqi woman I met after she escaped to the United States told me about a sniper who nearly killed her in 2006. "But because it was not my hour of death, I moved my head and the bullet passed by my ear," she said. This same woman told me about her neighbor in Baghdad taken by insurgents from a street corner. "She was raped and then dropped at the same spot where she was kidnapped. She is forever shamed," she said. Countless stories of Iraqi women trapped between al-Qaeda and security forces helped explain why some chose violence as an alternative to shame and a senseless death.

My research has shown that the primary individual motivation for women is personal: the protection of family, community, and country in order to bring about meaningful change to conflict. Studies of women in secular pan-Arab movements showed that women helped their men succeed: they collected funds, cooked and distributed food to soldiers, and published propaganda in their homes; some joined men in military combat. Female activists like Zangana believe that women in national movements liberate themselves by fighting alongside men. In the 1990s, before religious terrorism was a global threat, I studied the women of Algeria who fought in the Battle of Algiers to oppose French colonial rule. These women were instrumental to the war in 1958–1964 but returned to their homes after the independence of the Algerian state. Thus, women determined to change their community and country with violent action soon realized that their participation had no effect on empowering their gender.

Furthermore, Muslim women today often cite the early examples of female fighters but misplace their own struggles within a historical narrative that fails to explain *contextual pressures*, a term coined by Dr. Karla Cunningham that refers to the impact of domestic and international enforcement, conflict, and social dislocation. In the early battles, Muslim women did not enjoy equal status with men until a woman from the Quraysh aristocracy, Umm Salama, one day asked the Prophet, "Why are men mentioned in the Quran and why are we not?" Her reply came in the form of a verse: "Lo! Men who surrender unto Allah, and women who surrender to Allah, and men who believe and women who believe, and men who obey, and women who obey. . . . Allah hath prepared for them forgiveness and a vast reward."[4] This verse alone revolutionized the Muslim community, illuminating a break with pre-Islamic practices, and called into question the customs that ruled relations between the sexes.

The unintentional debate that women in conflict arouse is plastic; no conflict today has elevated the status of the Muslim woman or attempted to address the societal and religious norms that solidify the role of the Muslim woman. While her participation in suicide attacks serves the overall group or social movement, her individual contribution is seldom recognized, except in martyrdom fests where female bombers are deemed necessary for operational and strategic adaptation against a well-armed adversary. In other cases, women are expendable and a riding wave of al-Qaeda's success, a point I have made in lectures delivered at home and at international events. Their recruitment by men and other women makes them victims of violence. In some cases, these females are manipulated, trapped by the terror organization to do its dirty work. With no place to go, exploited females are pawns of delusion and deceit.

※

In August 2008, in the city of Baquba, northeast of Baghdad, in Diyala Province, a young female bomber stumbled along a dusty street in an oversized blue dress with pink and yellow flowers along the front border, her wavy brown hair covered in a black hijab. She had one task: go near the police checkpoint and detonate the bomb under her abaya. But the sixteen-year-old Rania Ibrahim couldn't do it. One year later, she was sentenced to seven years in prison for an attempted suicide attack.

Iraqi police released a video of Ibrahim, tied to a black steel bracket alongside a dirt road with the sun in her eyes as male officers cut off the multiple wires of the detonator that attached around her waist. Some say Ibrahim was drugged, which explained why she looked distracted, distressed, and disturbed.

The acting police chief, General Abdul Karim Khalaf, instructed an Iraqi police cameraman to capture the unstrapping of the female bomber, aired on Iraqi television, using a long metal pointer to show exactly what happened to the girl that the police discovered. As they detached the suicide vest packed with eighteen kilograms of explosives, men in police uniforms wearing helmets and bulletproof vests did what was unthinkable in a conservative Muslim society: they treated the young would-be suicide bomber like an exhibit to gain international attention and approval. One journalist told me that she believed Iraqi authorities had Ibrahim filmed before and after her arrest, including hours that she remained in police custody, as evidence of Iraq's ability to disrupt al-Qaeda. The police parade of Ibrahim may have been intended to alert the world community that local security forces could contain the threat of suicide terrorism.

Nothing could be further from the truth.

The statement that Ibrahim gave while in police custody revealed a network of other women with violent ambitions. She told the police that a relative had put the vest on her. She was told to wait outside for further instructions. She did not know what was happening to her. The details of Ibrahim's early life helped explain why she was an "unwilling suicide bomber," a description used by the US military.

There are varying accounts of what may have caused Ibrahim to not pull the wire. What we do know is this: she was born into a poor Sunni family; she left school when she was eleven years old; five months before her arrest, she was married to an al-Qaeda man in his twenties, whose own mother and aunt were members of the violent organization. Ibrahim was fifteen when her terrorist husband encouraged her to strap on the bomb. "We'll meet in Heaven," he said to her.

Ibrahim was smart when she staggered along the dust-filled road, calling attention to herself from the police manning a checkpoint. Perhaps it was her outsized and baggy abaya, too bulky for a girl of her small size. Or it could have been her half-conscious state that caused the police to question where she was going. Whatever it was, Ibrahim "saved" herself from dying, at least for a few hours more, until she would be sent to an Iraqi prison, where girls and women are often abused, raped, and tortured.

In conflicts around the world, men manipulate underage girls. But in Ibrahim's case, it was the women in her family who were the abusers: women with a political agenda or a personal vendetta. And the young Ibrahim was their redemption.

I learned about her arrest from Anita McNaught, the first Western journalist to gain access to Iraq's youngest female terrorist. I remember the morning that McNaught called me on a satellite phone. I had made another round of chai and stood in my kitchen. My kids were in school, and aside from the woodpecker outside, I reveled in the sound of silence. But that phone call changed everything I thought I knew about female bombers in the Islamic world.

"She did not want to kill anyone," McNaught said to me, confident that the young girl sitting on the rug in front of her was not

interested in al-Qaeda. McNaught was not alone with the failed
suicide bomber. In her personal notes, which she titled "On the
Sofa With a Human Bomb," she wrote,

> When I reached the office of the Police Chief, the frenzy was
> only starting. There was palpable excitement in the corridors.
> When the officers opened the door, we almost fell in. We were
> the first press, and the only Western media present. And the
> Acting Chief of Police was absolutely delighted with what his
> men had sprung him that day. Over the course of the next two
> hours, the room filled with Iraqi journalists, photographers
> and video cameras. It was a circus.[5]

McNaught shared the room with Iraqi police interrogators,
interpreters, and her own camera crew, trying to grasp how Ibrahim had strapped on the bomb. According to her story, the young
girl's in-laws placed the vest around her waist. The wires alarmed
her, she said. The women ordered Ibrahim to take the suicide vest
to her mother's home.

A female police officer leaned in to ask Ibrahim an ironic question. "So, you were taking it to your mother's so *she* could blow herself up?" McNaught said the girl took little notice of the officer.

She described the failed bomber as street-savvy. She had "a
self-possession beyond her years. She was nervous . . . she chewed
her bottom lip. But she met your gaze strongly and managed a wry
smile. She handled a burgeoning Iraqi media scrum in the police
chief's office with some dignity and when pressed by various inter-
locutors, pushed back crossly. Still, she gave little away—and even
less that would implicate her in the planned murder in which she
was intended to play a central role."

The real perpetrators were Ibrahim's mother, aunt, and sister-
in-law. All Ibrahim had to do was transport the suicide vest, and
she hoped that her mother "would sort out the problem for her—
perhaps by taking the vest to that very same checkpoint and turn
it in." The Arabic-language newspaper *Dar Al-Hayat* reported that
Major General Abd al-Kareem Khalaf, the commander of central
operations at the Ministry of Interior and acting Baquba police

commander, said the girl's mother was caught at home with an explosive vest and the girl's husband ran away.

McNaught told me that Ibrahim had no intention of hurting innocent people but was just the kind of female recruit that al-Qaeda looked for: She was young. She had little to no economic or social capital. She had a minimal education. She was born a Sunni Muslim and poor. Looking into Ibrahim's background, I felt a hollowness inside as if something were missing, something I could not name. The girl that al-Qaeda chose as their next victim wanted more for her life than an explosion. "It sounded to me that she had grown up in an environment where the dividing line between what you lived for and what you died for had become very blurred," McNaught told me. Ibrahim lived in a house with more than one suicide vest lying around. When police entered the house, they arrested the sisters-in-law and found another suicide vest.

During her arrest, Ibrahim told reporters that her father and elder brother had been kidnapped and murdered by military men in the past year. For the young girl, death had been normalized and suicide was a desired act rewarded by Paradise. But there was nothing conventional about suicide terrorism for Ibrahim. Her story revealed the ugly truth of al-Qaeda's strategy: the group snared girls and women into its dungeon of violence because it could.

On camera, the young would-be suicide bomber appeared unusually composed. McNaught was surprised at how confident Ibrahim seemed after having been publicly shamed as men removed her dress to deactivate the bomb, how calm she was when she was seated on a worn rug swarmed by journalists at the police station hours after her arrest. I considered for a moment that the illiterate girl might have believed she was free from the attack that would have ended her life. But she may not have considered what would happen next. Time spent in an Iraqi prison would not heal Ibrahim but might scar her—male police officers used rape to dishonor and disgrace female prisoners. "She may be better off dead," an Iraqi expert told me.

McNaught's description of Ibrahim's tragedy—a girl forced to put on a suicide vest by her own family—highlights the importance of relationships. In researching the lives of female terrorists, I have come to the following conclusion: most girls and women lost close male relatives; they lived under radical teachings dictated by violent men or women; and girls may have no control over their own lives, including the choice of marriage. Ibrahim may have been too young and naïve to have rebelled against her family. *What could she have done?* I thought. It was unclear whether she wanted to run away; if she had, where could she have gone in war-torn Iraq? Who would protect her? In many cases, girls have no option except to obey the orders of their elders.

While Ibrahim did not choose the violent path, other women entered terrorism willingly. Psychologists point to certain event factors to explain why and how some girls and women self-select for suicide operations. Trauma is a key motivator that is determined by the following: the level of exposure a female has to a violent event; her age at the time of the event; being a victim of multiple traumatic incidents; the duration of the trauma; the existence of an ongoing threat that the trauma will continue; and so on. Suicide terrorism is a choice that is explained by feelings of helplessness; a tendency toward risk-taking; and an intense anger, resulting in harm to others as well as self-harm. My mentor Dr. Post has spent a lifetime examining what lies behind the behavior of suicide terrorists.

In our conversations, I have learned to accept that each woman's story is unique and to be willing to say, "Who knows?" when asked about motive for every female who has committed a violent act. As novelist D. H. Lawrence said, the soul is a dark forest.

When I was in my twenties, barely intelligent enough to pursue the study of terrorism, I learned the danger of fragmentation. Canadian adventure writer Robert Young Pelton, who risks his life to find the truth in internecine wars, reminded me that the female terrorist is more than a news story. Her flirtation with death and strange infatuation with violence is more than grist for a Hollywood thriller. If there's anything I've learned from my gurus, it's that the seemingly seductive lives of female terrorists are closer to mundane accounts of repugnant psychopaths; only in recent years have females, the object of swooning attention by the international community, left their homes on a forbidden passionate adventure, the Western girls of ISIS among them.

Perhaps they believe that their love for martyrdom—the kill perceived as the ultimate individual choice made by women—will allow them to translate their anger into so-called meaningful action. They choose the right to die, to attain spiritual reward, a general vulgarity disguised as divine intervention. Over time, the stories of female bombers, including those who have failed, are confined in a living anthology and become the subject of television.

The more I looked at Ibrahim, the more I came to believe that saying no to her young terrorist husband had not been an option. For most females drawn or forced into violent groups, there is no turning back. They join violent men to fulfill their own personal desire for marriage and to satisfy the need for change, the result of which is the opposite of change: more violence leading to a cycle of carnage. For some women, the pursuit of violence is explained by raw revenge rather than an affirmation of faith.

An imprisoned Iraqi would-be suicide bomber, Baida Abdul Karim al-Shammari, the mother of two boys and a girl, said in an interview that she was ready to "explode [the Americans] because they are invaders and blasphemers and Jewish. I will explode them first because . . . they feel free to take our lands." Al-Shammari's motive was simple: "to take revenge on her brothers' killers—American soldiers," reported Alissa J. Rubin in the *New York Times*. The would-be bomber also remembered the shooting of a neighbor in the back of the neck by the US military in 2005. "I saw him running toward them, and then they shot him in the neck. I still see him. . . . I saw him clawing on the ground in the dust before his soul left his body. After that I began to help with making improvised explosive devices."[6] Al-Shammari and Ibrahim shared a jail cell after their arrests in Baquba, forty miles northeast of Baghdad, Iraq's segregated capital city.

Religious-inspired terrorism lives in a permanent contradiction: its idea of Islam as the solution is a sacred value, yet its vision of violence in the name of God entails its transformation into a political belief that delights in evil for its own sake. The image and perception of female terrorists as frighteningly cold and conscienceless offers no meaning or understanding. Rather, it creates distance and distrust, which makes studying the actions and motivations of these women and girls nearly impossible. As a researcher, I had to separate the distorted faith preached by extremists from the peaceful practice of Islam in order to understand that some women and girls don't act in the name of religion at all. It is the male terrorist who uses scripture to achieve a political end. Except that in this case, Ibrahim and Al-Shammari didn't join al-Qaeda for political or religious reasons.

It was personal. Ibrahim's Aunt Wijdan recruited females. Her father and brother were found making bombs for al-Qaeda. They used Ibrahim for a suicide mission, and the young girl said she hadn't known. There are conflicting reports about Ibrahim's intention to kill or not to kill. Her cellmate, Al-Shammari, believed that the young girl knew exactly what she was doing. When she was outfitted with the suicide vest, Ibrahim claimed that "there were red wires, but I didn't know what was inside it." Although Ibrahim appeared untrained for suicide, Al-Shammari was prepared. Dubbed the "bad mother," she helped make bombs, buying wires and other parts. "We are doing it for God's sake. We are doing it as jihad," she told the *Times*. Both women had married young, and in Al-Shammari's case, her husband regularly beat her. As of this writing, their husbands are believed to be dead.

Around the same time, Iraqi police arrested Samira Ahmed Jassim, a prime terrorist recruiter of Iraqi girls and women. The arrest of Jassim in January 2009 was a breakthrough for Iraqi authorities, who had begun to realize the gravity of women's roles in terrorist groups. Nicknamed "Mother of the Believers" or Umm al-Mumineen, Jassim had recruited eighty women as suicide operatives, twenty-eight of whom had launched successful attacks. A spokesman for Baghdad operations, Kassem Atta, confirmed that Jassim belonged to the terrorist group Ansar al Sunna, taking orders from a Muslim cleric through an intermediary named Shaker. Her primary role was to encourage vulnerable females to carry out attacks.

In pictures, Jassim looked to be around fifty, her hair and body covered in all-black fabric. In a filmed confession, Jassim described the recruitment process: she found girls who had been traumatized by the war, rape victims, females with family problems, and/or those with signs of depression. Her first female recruit, Um Huda, detonated in a police station in Makdadia, located northeast of Baghdad; her second recruit was an old, unmarried woman who exploded in the same city; and so on. After Jassim's arrest, Iraqi and American authorities began to recognize that women played a vital role in violent groups. Without them, I argue, male-dominated groups could not survive.

Outside of operations, females are chief propagandists. After a drone strike killed Al-Zarqawi in 2006, his wife, Umm Muhammad, posted a communiqué online calling on all Muslim men to avenge the death of her husband. "We are all Zarqawi," she wrote. It was her way of shaming other Muslim men, those not yet in arms, and to seek worldwide support for the men dedicated to destroying the West and its allies. Three years later, Umayma Hasan, the wife of the former al-Qaeda leader in Iraq, released a letter identifying three kinds of Muslim women: fighters, sisters in Islam in prison, and the rest. She wrote, "I will advise my Muslim sisters to impart in their sons the love of jihad and the will to serve it." Before her, in the late 1980s, the wife of al-Qaeda's spiritual guide, Abdullah Azzam, wrote in her memoir, "I ask my Muslim sisters to encourage their husbands and sons to continue with the jihad."

As war raged on in Iraq, ISIS besieged Fallujah in January 2014 and captured Mosul and Tikrit a few months later. The group's swift expansion of power and territory bolstered al-Baghdadi, who followed al-Zarqawi's example by welcoming women into its global movement. ISIS needed wives and mothers. Only a few would take up arms.

ISIS calls on women from all countries to join its post-national, post-racial community structured on an unreal version of Islam. American Muslim scholar Haroon Moghul denounced ISIS as anything but Muslim. "Its relationship to Islam is like Frankenstein to a human being, or a zombie to a living person," he told CNN. Violent extremists like ISIS violate Islamic history and theology. They pervert the Prophetic model from seventh-century Arabia in which Muhammad called for peace, love, and mercy, rather than war, hate, and intolerance.

Islamic or not, ISIS portrays itself as an equal opportunity organization. Male recruiters prey on females online and offline, encouraging participation as protectorates of the new state. The females of ISIS offer the same emotional, spiritual, and physical support to their men. By joining, women belong to a collective identity that promises them pride and purpose. They share men's personal and political reasons to kill the enemy. More important, women lead by example, encouraging other females to commit to the group's ideological fervor, organizational goals, and national ambition.

Today, the women of ISIS are like al-Qaeda: they are calculated, committed, and compassionate toward the group and its objectives. The modern *muhajiraat*, or migrants, are equally deceptive in their Western clothing, accents, and upbringing. But once assimilated into ISIS territory, women lose their individuality; they are unrecognizable in all-black robes, gloves, and matching fabric over their faces. To the outside world, the females have disappeared, forever lost to an uncertain future governed by men with guns. As Western women began to leave for Syria, I considered for a moment. *Will they be happy in their new home?* We know from multiple media reports, Twitter accounts, and ongoing data collection that the women of Raqqa have mixed emotions about their new roles and responsibilities.

Whatever their role, this is a threat we can't ignore. Without women, ISIS or any other violent group will not survive. Without female recruits, ISIS cannot call for a Caliphate. No Muslim community is made by men, alone. If only women could see that joining violent groups guarantees a chaotic present, rather than a promising future. What these girls do not know is that the fantasy and friendship they desire from radicals in Islam could lead to danger and death.

The ultimate deception is chasing a dream unfulfilled.

# Chapter Four

# THE STRANGER

## *San Bernardino, California*

She was a stranger to most people, including her own family. On December 2, 2015, a twenty-something young woman named Tashfeen Malik from Pakistan and her husband, Syed Farook, gunned down fourteen people and wounded others in one of the deadliest mass shootings in America. Masked in black, her face concealed, the girl from Pakistan assaulted my religion.

In the first hour of the attack, I wondered aloud if Malik would be hated less if she sported a painted leather jacket, low-rise jeans, and leather boots. If she had appeared more Western, rather than hidden from the public's view, she might have been accepted as a Muslim woman. Interviews with Western women confirm that they perceive Muslim women draped in dark garb, including the covering of their eyes, as anonymous or nonexistent. One American woman said to me, "I can't talk to her if I can't see her as a person."

I wanted to believe that Malik's religion did not matter. Even when it did. I knew that Islam would come under attack again by those who did not understand it because a Muslim woman ruined the lives of innocent Americans and put Islam in the spotlight. Again.

I watched the news in horror. My phone began to ring. Emails poured in from journalists wanting to know: *How can a Muslim woman do this?* In a cracked voice, I responded, as I had for the past fifteen years, "This is not my religion." I did not know what the Pakistani-born woman believed she would accomplish by killing Americans in the name of Islam, ISIS, and possibly her gender.

When the names and faces of the victims flashed across the television screen—representing families who had lost a father, mother, brother, sister, child, or friend—I began to wonder if Malik fit into my simple Three Cs model. The first C had to do with context. Were there *contextual clues*, such as exposure to trauma, violence, or abuse, or did she have feelings of rage, anxiety, or depression that might explain her behavior? We can't assume that Malik exhibited emotional problems, though she did alienate herself from the community to which she belonged. That no one knew who she really was made her a stranger among friends and family.

The second C focused on culture: the customs, traditions, and religious ideology that affect an individual's childhood and his or her relations with the family and the community. Was Malik a victim or a champion (or protector or defender) of her *culture*? I knew from travels to Pakistan that most extremist men do not choose women to kill, but rather, women play a secondary role, which meant the cultural piece did not make sense. The third C explored an individual's capability, which included the willingness to support or participate in extreme violence. In this case, Malik proved herself *capable*. But how and when she trained to use a weapon, and by whom, is still a mystery. According to public reports, all we know is that Malik knew how to kill in cold blood and may have had practice with target shooting.

Once again, I was compelled to speak *for* Islam and *against* violence in the name of my religion. After Malik's attack, I received calls from the media. I told MSNBC and the Associated Press that Islam is a religion of mercy, peace, and compassion. That no pious, practicing Muslim would gun down innocent people. That killing is sinful, senseless, and Satanic. That the Quran made it explicitly clear that whoever saves a life saves all of humanity. That the Prophet of Islam once said that the gates of Heaven will be forever closed to one who takes a life in a suicide mission. However, extremists like Malik practiced Islam selectively and referenced religious verse out of context to suit their deadly actions.

In truth, Malik's case is not as bizarre as it seems. There is a history of women in violent groups. I told MSNBC that what surprised me was that Malik assumed an operational role, which was uncommon for most extremist women. Many radical women are supporters, sympathizers: they help their men evade arrests, they keep their secrets, they feed their accomplices, they raise their children to become extremists, and much more. But so few actually learn how to kill, as Malik did, which raises questions: Where did she receive weapons training? Who trained her? Was there anyone else, aside from her husband, who had radicalized her? When had she become an extremist—before or after she arrived at Los Angeles International Airport?

Days later, security personnel announced on television that Malik had been radicalized for years. "This attack was planned for two years. . . . [Malik came from] a network from Pakistan." "Yes, that's plausible," I told a Canadian reporter, when she asked me about the Islamic school that Malik had attended.

Soon enough, reporters suggested that Malik—like many other radicalized women—had led a normal life before she became a terrorist. This isn't so unusual, either. No woman (or man) enters extremism without motive. However, in Malik's case, investigators in December 2016, a year after the attack, were still clueless as to *how* she had turned violent.

*Why now?* The simple answer is that it's complicated and complex. No two terrorists are alike, although there are patterns and trends that can explain, in part, why religious extremism is increasing. And there is a list of likely motivations that terrorism experts use as a guide to understand the reasons why ordinary Muslims are radicalized and commit the most extraordinary attacks. To be fair, religious-based violence is an old phenomenon that dates back to early Islamic history; some scholars cite the killing of Ali, a cousin and son-in-law of Prophet Muhammad, by another Muslim as the first "terror" attack. Other significant deaths of pious Muslims occurred after Muhammad's death—his two grandsons, Hussein and Hassan, were both brutally slaughtered at the order of a man named Mawiya, who ruled a stretch of land that later became Syria. Rulers justified violence in the name of Islam, though there was no justification for it in the Quran. The leaders were simply motivated by greed and power.

Later that December day, Mama called to express her shock and sorrow. "It's terrible," she said. "Can you believe she was from Punjab?"

"Yes, I know; Punjabi women are anything but radical." A frequent traveler to Pakistan, I know that Punjabi women in cities and major towns are known to be progressive and liberal-minded. They are politicians, peacemakers, playwrights, pilots, police officers, poets, and more. In my own family, I have women who are star-crazed fashion designers, successful entrepreneurs, and award-winning educators.

They are anything but mass murderers.

As a lecturer and researcher, I have learned that the radicalization process is devoid of categories or a step-by-step process. There is no how-to guide or "aha" moment. Nor is there a one-size-fits-all model. Which is why it's useless and unnecessary to place violent women in classification boxes and create profiles. It doesn't work. Instead, each woman's entry into a terrorist group is unique because no two Muslim women are alike.[1]

The threat of women wishing to die for a cause is real. Decades of female participation on the front lines of terror have proved that women can be deadly. Women are determined and devoted to a cause they volunteer for or have been recruited into by male handlers. These women are young and old, secular and religious, married and single, or widows. Even mothers are motivated by a message of resistance, rebellion, and revenge. These women belong to a larger network of extremists who stress the need for justice, a narrative that resonates for women. According to Dr. Post, women usually radicalize for "altruistic" reasons: they express a desire to fight social injustice, some leave behind their own children to save future generations from real or perceived aggression, and many believe that violence is the *only* way to save the Muslim world.

Malik was the perfect stranger. She was no different than other Muslim women who slipped by intelligence and law enforcement officers when they entered America. I am reminded of the Pakistani woman Aafia Siddiqui, who made the FBI's Most Wanted List for her relationship to senior terrorists including Khalid Shaykh Muhammad, who was a high-value target captured in a safe house in Pakistan and indicted on countless terrorism charges.

For years, Aafia Siddiqui did not concern us. When she studied at MIT in Boston, Siddiqui became an ardent supporter of wars in the Islamic world, including Bosnia, Chechnya, and Afghanistan. She rallied for innocent Muslims killed in the line of fire and vocally attacked countries for attacking Muslim lands. Years later, she was captured in Pakistan, where she allegedly disappeared until she suddenly showed up in Afghanistan and was arrested for attacking US military officers. Siddiqui was tried in New York for the alleged crime and then sent to serve her life sentence in Texas.

In Pakistan, thousands of people protested Siddiqui's arrest and trial in America. For many, she was a heroine of Islam, and her supporters, including her own family, believed that she had been misjudged and mislabeled a terrorist. Pakistanis do not nurture the same feelings for Malik, whose barbaric act shamed the country from which she came.

In truth, Siddiqui was not the first Muslim woman who called on men to defend the rights of Muslims, though her case is highly controversial. Her sympathizers and family members believe that she didn't join al-Qaeda willingly, and if she did, it was fate. Others insist that Siddiqui is a hardened terrorist and more dangerous than men—that she has the ability to deceive local and foreign authorities and disguise her intention to support and commit acts of violence. To this day, protesters organize outside the prison in Texas where Siddiqui is held and demand her release, according to an American security officer whom I met at a law enforcement event. If there's one thing I have learned from Siddiqui's case, it is that Muslim women continue to be perceived as victims of conflict rather than victimizers. Despite Siddiqui's links with senior al-Qaeda operatives, many consider her to be a martyr—the ultimate sufferer—in the war on terrorism.

However, history offers evidence of women on the front lines of war. During the Afghan jihad, women supported their men with logistics and facilitation. I know this from dozens of articles I collected with my father, a linguist and translator. We surfed through

Urdu-language magazine articles, some written by women, many
written for women, on their role in jihad. In one editorial, a woman
said, "We stand shoulder to shoulder with our men, supporting
them, helping them . . . we educate their sons and we prepare ourselves . . . we march in the path of jihad for the sake of Allah, and our
goal is Shahada [martyrdom]." Years later, women clad in all-black
robes with matching gloves, their faces shielded by cloth, protested
with banners on the streets of Islamabad, Pakistan's capital city,
and claimed their right to take over the city with violence. A local
newspaper, the *Daily Times*, reported that the women justified their
action against "those who are against Islam" because they were an
"oppressed community."

In Pakistan, male extremists and their leaders often manipulate
women to win political attention and public sympathy. Their defiance of and disgust for the United States–led war on terrorism is a
win-win: some men use this narrative to appeal to women who have
little access to education and opportunities. In a personal interview
with a former minister of information and the editor of a major
newspaper, I was told that these women "are docile and under the
subjugation of men; they are exploited by the *maulvis* [religious
leaders] to challenge authorities [the state] and create fear."

To be fair, the majority of mosques and religious schools in
Pakistan do not incite violence or terrorism. A Muslim country,
Pakistan has a history of secular politics—religious parties have
never gained the majority of the vote in elections, nor do they have
wide support across a moderate Muslim population. However, it
is entirely possible that the San Bernardino shooter was radicalized in Pakistan by violent extremist groups before she entered the
United States.

During the Malik investigation, I was asked about the Al-Huda
University in Islamabad, run by a woman, Farhat Hashmi, who was
educated in Scotland and earned her doctoral degree in Islamic
studies at the University of Glasgow. When she returned to Pakistan, she founded Al-Huda to teach girls the meaning of the Quran.
Her teachings are considered stringent. With nearly seventy
schools across Pakistan, Hashmi is spreading a conservative ideology that secularists, liberals, and moderate Muslims perceive to

be controversial and a viewpoint that restricts the rights of women and girls in Islam. In an interview with *CBC News*, I told a reporter, "When you learn about religion from a narrow lens . . . then you tend to have a less tolerant view of the world." Before she committed mass murder, Malik attended the Al-Huda branch in the city of Multan in Pakistan while she studied pharmacology at a local university, a course she never completed.

The rigid teachings of Islam are all too familiar. Although Malik is the first Pakistani woman to shoot Americans, she represents a wider and more disturbing trend of an uncompromising Islamic scholarship spreading in the Muslim and Western worlds. The students of Al-Huda reminded me of the girls I met years ago at the largest girls' *madrasa*, or religious seminary, in Quetta, the home of one-eyed Mullah Omar, the Taliban's revered founder. There, I sat cross-legged on a rug talking to teachers who had all joined the school at the age of eight. In a short piece published in the travel section of the *Washington Post*, I wrote, "Behind the iron gates, girls as young as eight memorized the Quran; they also mended clothes and cooked their own food. 'Don't you want to see life outside of the school?' I asked a young teacher. Her response still stings me. 'Of course we have desires, but we learn to suppress them.'"[2]

My sharpest memory of that place was a young bright-eyed girl who sang religious songs. In ultraconservative Islam, it is forbidden to appear in front of unknown men, much less perform for them. But in the Quetta madrasa, the girl was honored for praising God's name. Even so, I often wondered how the girls of the school felt about being confined within the walls of the madrasa. Did they want to go shopping? Or eat in a restaurant? Did they want to go to a secular/public school? Or just ride a bicycle outside? I was struck by the girls' complacency, mistaken for gratitude they felt for their male leader.

One wintry afternoon, as we huddled together on the floor, I tried to teach the girls Islam. I told them the story of the Prophet's first love, a woman named Khadija, who was fifteen years older, a successful businesswoman, and a widow. I referenced Islamic scripture to show the girls that they had the right to be free, think, and act of their own will.

"We have each other," a seventeen-year-old teacher said to me in private, referring to the other girls, whom she considered her friends. And then I understood that an ultraconservative teaching of Islam was what allowed the girls to leave their homes. It meant something to them. Until they joined the madrasa, most of the girls had lived in seclusion—they were illiterate and ignorant of faith. As I smiled back at them, I began to understand how easy it is to accept a narrow version of religion as an opening to a new life while being oblivious to Islam's truth. These girls had no clue that Islam afforded them the right to study, work, go to a movie, sing or dance (with other girls), and fall in love.

Behind the stone-gray walls, the girls looked happy. They had each other. A teacher with rosy cheeks and swan-white skin told me she would rather stay in the madrasa than return home for the holidays. I imagine that if I had been raised in their village and culture, I might have chosen to stay in the madrasa too, and rejoice in the company of friends rather than have to return to a patronizing father.

In the early days of Islam, Muslim women helped their men to victory. They tended to wounded soldiers. They carried messages and money. They called on men to fight to protect Muhammad. They were the mothers of the believers.[3] Women were skilled in warfare. They were given swords to use in fighting by the early Muslim men. One of the most celebrated female fighters was Nusybah bint Ka'ab, also known as Umm Umarah ("mother of Umarah"). She fought in Islam's second Battle of Uhud in 625 CE, lost one arm, and suffered eleven wounds as she protected her Prophet.[4] After Muhammad's death, Muslim women continued to fight. A Bedouin woman, Khawlah bint al-Azwar, dressed like a knight and entered the battlefield with other women. She "slashed the head of the Greek," a reference to the Byzantines who retreated after Muslims declared victory.[5]

In the spirit of faith, the first *mujahidaat*, or female fighters, were elevated by the Prophet as the most noble of women. Only those who sacrificed their lives in defense of their honor, their homes, or Prophet Muhammad would be remembered. These women were entitled to Heaven for their contribution in war. They were celebrated as martyrs of the faith. Under Islamic law, Malik could not qualify as a martyr because she had killed innocent people, for which there is no passage to Paradise.

Despite her narrow lens on the world, Malik didn't seem out of the ordinary to anyone, although there should have been behavioral clues to alert the community and the police. In Malik's case, Muslims at the mosque didn't know her. Her own brother-in-law professed on national television that he had never seen her face. For an American, this seems absurd. I have told reporters that even in strict Islamic households, women let down their hair and show their face to male relatives. How could a woman living in our neighborhoods *not* socialize with her family members, much less other Americans?

Ultraconservative Islam is not uncommon in the United States. In many Muslim families living in the West, a girl is expected to marry young and start her own family. I am familiar with many girls who lead parallel lives in America; living in ultraconservative families, they struggle to fit in, and few adjust to the values in the dominant culture in which they are raised. I know a sixteen-year-old girl who is not allowed to leave the house without being accompanied by one of her parents or brother. She wears the *niqab*, a full-length veil that covers her body and her face, everything except her eyes. She is home-schooled, and her parents are looking for a groom as I write this, which means she will probably get married before she is twenty, like her elder sister, who had an arranged marriage. It's also likely that a teenage girl in Virginia will do exactly as she is told, obeying fixed gender norms set by her parents, who follow one narrow version of Islam. Although this young girl is not an extremist, her restricted life and narrow worldview make her a vulnerable target.

In addition to the crimes she committed, Malik also reinforced the traditional sexual stereotype of a Muslim woman as a home-bound housewife, who is likely oppressed and ostracized from the world. To the American public, she looked like the orthodox

Muslim woman devoid of freedom. Nothing could be further from the truth, as Malik proved to be an equal accomplice with her terrorist husband.

Will there be another Malik? My answer is "I hope not," though I can't be sure, when extremist women, like men, live among us. Reporting radicals to authorities is an important first step toward keeping America safe. In the fight against violent extremism, numerous American Muslims have reported suspicious activities to law enforcement officers to disrupt attacks against the homeland. Ron Haddad, the chief of police for Dearborn, Michigan— often referred to as the "Arab capital of North America," with its swelling population of Arab Muslims—acknowledges the help he has received from Muslims.

In an effort to improve community policing and relations with the American Muslim community, the FBI started a program called "Shared Responsibility Committees" in November 2015. The purpose of these committees was to bring together law enforcement officers, mental health professionals, social workers, and imams and other religious leaders to create meaningful and effective intervention strategies. The program was controversial, as such a high level of engagement with local Muslim communities to fight terrorism in the United States is unprecedented. Other efforts by the federal government were also geared toward reducing the number of alienated Muslim youth drawn to ISIS and other terrorist groups through extremist propaganda and offline networks.

In 2016, I met with Hedieh Mirahmadi, a Muslim activist and lawyer based in Montgomery County, Maryland, who supports the FBI's outreach efforts to engage the Muslim youth before it's too late. Of Iranian descent, born in Chicago and raised in Los Angeles, Mirahmadi moved to the Washington, DC, area in 1997 and founded WORDE, a nongovernmental organization committed to empowering the community with educational tools and resources to fight against extremists at home and abroad.

I first met Mirahmadi when I was a young government analyst, and we reconnected years later at a conference on radical women, held at the Center for Strategic International Studies. She invited me to her home, a palatial space with a majestic Quran and antique furniture, and talked about her work over tea and a fruit tart.

"I had a series of pivotal events," she recalled. "I came across what I considered to be nefarious groups that didn't have the best interests of America at heart, and not the best interests of Muslims at heart. The 1990s was a time when some people had an anti-pluralistic and anti-American approach to Islam that concerned me. It almost led me to leave Islam. So I found a different group of people very much tied to Sufism, but my concern and passion about this issue . . . never went away. I spent countless hours interviewing young Muslims trying to understand what was drawing them to go and fight in faraway lands. So many felt that there was a struggle for the soul of Islam, and it was very pronounced in America."

Like Mirahmadi, I remember growing up in the 1990s. Conflicts in the Muslim world continued to shape the way American Muslims reacted. The long, drawn-out war in Afghanistan with the Soviet Union had just come to an end, sparking the rise of violent extremists that would spill into Pakistan. We both agreed that the threat, twenty years later, was the same but the dynamics had changed.

"Are you concerned about extremism in America?" I asked her; this was a few months before Tashfeen Malik terrorized the San Bernardino community.

"The recruitment patterns have changed," she replied. "It's not in person and not in the mosque. Today, it's in third spaces, and groups have changed; they are not calling everyone to go to war overseas."

*Which is why ISIS recruits women like Malik. They are looking for local Muslims to conduct local attacks, similar to the sequence of attacks that are taking place in European cities,* I thought.

"All those things have changed," she continued, "but the fundamental issue that remains is how do you build resilience of communities against that? American Muslims need a version of their religion that is not incompatible with being American. The message that terrorism has no place in Islam resonates, and now American Muslims are more courageous to condemn the violence. The message that American Muslims can be loyal citizens to this country and violent extremists are deviants of mainstream Islamic practice is finally being heard, but there is still work to be done."

Under her guidance, WORDE is creating the space for local communities to become active participants in public safety. Since 2008, the organization has provided training to thousands of community members, including other faith-based leaders and members, to encourage inclusion, tolerance, and awareness of the dangers of violent extremism.

"Our goal is to build awareness by helping the community look at risk factors and potential drivers of violence," she said. "The key factors are psychological, sociological, economic, and ideological beliefs."

The matrix sounded familiar. Borrowing from other models, Mirahmadi understands that there are no profiles, but there are factors to help identify at-risk individuals, similar to those used for school shooters and gang members. Community members, including religious leaders, counselors, social workers, educators, and parents, use the matrix to help them engage with potential recruits *before* calling the police.

But for Malik and the San Bernardino community, there was no intervention and nothing to report, because Malik shielded herself from the mosque and the mainstream community—even when she went to the mosque, she prayed and returned home. People like Malik are an anomaly, a rare radical who attempts an attack and succeeds. To prevent another operative like Malik from attacking the United States, the community will need to be more vigilant. Though the Muslim community cannot keep an operative from entering the United States, which is the responsibility of law enforcement and immigration authorities, it is fair to expect the larger community to know its neighbors. I am reminded of the words of a young imam, who said to me, "We need to clean our own homes and strengthen our families."

We can no longer live by *not* knowing the stranger next door.

# Chapter Five

# WHERE THE GIRLS ARE

*Denver, Colorado*

On Friday, October 17, 2014, Assad Ibrahim, who was from Sudan, got a call from his daughter's school in Aurora, Colorado, a suburb of Denver. The calls are routine when parents fail to report an absence, or when a student arrives late or cuts class, at Overland High. His then-sixteen-year-old daughter had not come home. He called her cell phone and she answered. "I'm running late," she told him. But when she did not return after school, Ibrahim grew concerned. He discovered that his daughter's passport was missing. Where could she have gone?

Ibrahim visited the home of a friend, Farah Ali, a Somali immigrant who lived nearby with his family, and told him about his missing daughter. Had Ali seen his girls? The three were friends. Ali's daughters were seventeen and fifteen at the time. Ali said he had talked to them that morning while he was working. The two sisters said they were sick, but at 10:30 a.m. they felt well enough to go to the library. Ibrahim suggested that his friend look for their passports and the two thousand dollars that the family kept at the home—gone. The fathers called the FBI and filed runaway/missing-persons reports with the Arapahoe County Sheriff's Office. Desperate to find his daughter, one of the fathers posted on Twitter: "Please if you read this tell me where you are? We are so worried about you #Isis #raqqa #Colorado."

What Ibrahim couldn't possibly imagine was that his daughter and her friends were en route to Syria, a country none of them had seen and could only have imagined. Syria was far from home. Luckily for Ibrahim, the authorities tracked down their plane, heading to Frankfurt, Germany, from Chicago. The girls' plan was thwarted once the Germans were notified by the United States that the girls were on the run.

When apprehended at the airport, the girls told authorities that they were heading to Turkey to study. By the order of a judge, they were detained for a day by police in Frankfurt and then returned home to Colorado on Sunday. On Monday, the three girls were met at the airport in Denver by their parents and the FBI. Jeffrey Dorschner, the public information officer for the FBI and Department of Justice, said he hadn't heard about the incident until he got a call from a Turkish newspaper on Sunday night. He offered little more. Because the girls were underage and federal law considers crimes committed by minors as delinquency, the girls would not be charged or even named.

For the two families, who had assimilated into America, the radicalization of their daughters was unimaginable. Farah Ali had voted in the last two general elections. Assad Ibrahim told Colorado Public Radio, "My daughter did unbelievable, unthinkable things. I don't want any other person to go through this. If I didn't get her back, I don't know what would have happened to me." He added that his "heart fell down" when he got the news that his daughter had left to join ISIS. "I just felt something really bad is going to happen."

Unbeknownst to their families, the girls lived a very active online life, especially on Twitter. Authorities discovered that one of the sisters had sent nine thousand tweets over the previous month. In the days leading up to their departure, one of the girls tweeted, "I started to notice the people I called 'friends' weren't my true friends." The *Denver Post* discovered that just hours before they were reported missing, one girl posted this tweet: "Please please please make [prayer] for me wherever you are. I truly need it, may

Allah bless you all." In another tweet, she wrote: "Please make (prayer) for us three. It's extremely urgent." People from the United Kingdom and East Africa sent back tweets with words of encouragement and blessings.

It's not unusual that the girls used social media to talk about their travel plans. They didn't know that authorities were watching. Tustin Amole, who was the spokesperson for the Cherry Creek School District, said, "Students came in on Monday morning and reported the tweets to us. They said they were going to Germany and try to go to Turkey. Some of the students [on Twitter] told them it was a bad idea; others said good luck."[1] Amole added that the three teens had no prior issues at school, and the only thing on their record was unexcused absences. "There's no indication they had been radicalized in a way that they wanted to fight for ISIS. In most of these cases like this, it's not so much they want to fight with ISIS," she said. "They are promised they will have homes, be safe, have husbands, and live within their religion." The SITE Intelligence Group, which analyzed the girls' media accounts, reported that the three teens showed a shift toward extremism. On her blog site, director Rita Katz stated, "For a fifteen-year-old girl to have 9000 tweets means they are constantly online. When you see these numbers, you understand these girls lived their lives on social media."[2]

How could three teenage girls from a quiet suburb of Denver become radicalized? While the girls lived in an area that was sometimes called "Saudi Aurora" for all the Muslim immigrants who had settled there, it was a typical diverse middle-class community. In an area of East African immigrants, there was not a history of girls (or boys) joining Islamist-based terrorist groups. Hafedh Ferjani, the chairman of the Colorado Muslim Council, told the local CBS affiliate, "I was shocked because, according to our prediction, we thought the boys were easy targets. To our surprise, the girls were easy targets." Reports of Somali boys joining ISIS came from Minneapolis, which has the largest concentration of Somali immigrants in the United States. They hail from an area called "Little Mogadishu" and are pulled in by ISIS online. But that wasn't supposed to happen in suburban Denver.

Mohamed Nur, president of the Somali Community Center of Colorado, in Parker, Colorado, said he knew the two sisters. The girls came to America in 2004. The last time he saw them was in the spring before the after-school program ended. "They used to come and help the small kids," he said. In an interview with *NBC News*, Nur said the girls were part of a moderate Islamic community where there was no extremism. "Nobody knows what motivated them," Nur said. "We are a small community. We don't want attention. We are different in the way we dress. Who is the best medicine? We are the best medicine. We want the government, local government, and the state of Colorado to work with us and the center . . . we need youth activities because there is a gap." Nur envisioned a center with recreational activities, including sports, and counseling for the youth.

While the young girls involved in the incident have remained silent, some of their high school classmates talked about how the girls' actions had affected them. "I was shocked and scared at the same time," said then-fourteen-year-old Nimo Yousuf. "Some teens don't think of consequences. They just think of now." Her brother, then-seventeen-year-old Liban, said it was easy for young people to be lured online. "I think you look at their name. Look at the profile picture. I mean, if you see a black teen wearing a scarf and there it is. You could talk to them."

He added, "It's always easy to get in kids' mind. They are innocent. They don't know what's right from wrong, so you know you could tell them, come do this. This is the right way, and it could be easier for them to listen. I think it could happen anywhere, anywhere with kids." Another Somali student said the teens' flight was a wake-up call for the community. "One of the things that makes it scary is that if it's so easy for two or three little girls to go and almost get to wherever they're headed, then this could happen again and again. We have to focus on how to prevent it."

Before I left for Denver, a journalist named Vicky Collins encouraged me to learn more about the Muslim girls, who remain under the close watch of their parents. "You have to talk to the girls," Vicky said. "You're a Muslim. Maybe they will tell you their side of the story." Collins persuaded me to meet her in person and made me believe that I could gain access to the Muslim community in Denver in order to understand and further investigate the Muslim girls who had almost joined ISIS.

One cold morning, I drove to their home. *Bismillah. You don't know me, but* . . . This was the fourth door I would knock on, trying to find the Sudanese girl. I stood at the door of a townhouse with a child's bike parked along the wall. I talked to myself for a few minutes before I knocked on the door.

*Bismillah* (In the Name of God). *You don't know me, but I am a Muslim. I came here from another city. I only want to speak to you.*

A man in a long white garment called a *thaub* opened the door. A small boy tugged at his father's side. The man looked surprised and maintained a safe distance from me. As a Muslim woman, I had to allow for this awkward space, out of respect for the man I had just startled and for myself as a stranger.

"Who are you?" he asked, looking confused.

"I'm not a journalist. I'm not a reporter. I am just a woman here to learn about your daughter and what happened."

The man's eyes widened and he leaned back, clasping the doorknob. "We are not allowed to speak to you. I'm sorry."

"I am not a reporter," I repeated.

From media reports, I knew that this was the man who had alerted the authorities. He was the father who had saved his child and the Somali sisters from disappearing. To many, he was a hero for bringing the girls home.

In an interview with a local Denver news station, the Sudanese father said, "What they did is unacceptable, and they changed their lives, and they changed our lives. . . . She realizes she made a mistake."

With perfect composure, the father began to slide behind the doorway. "What happened was a year ago. It is over. My daughter can't talk to anyone. It's the rule. I am not allowed to talk to you. This is what they have told me. I'm sorry but I can't."

*Who are "they"? The attorney general? The police?* In that moment, I sensed a hint of fear and paranoia. While his daughter's emotions and thoughts were shrouded in mystery and a degree of suspicion, I know I would have done the same—protect my daughter from strangers.

And the door closed slowly.

Later that day, I learned that the Sudanese girl had not returned to school. The Somali sisters did. The community accepted them again and promised to protect them from harm. "We take care of each other," I was told, by a teenage friend of the two girls, which became a common theme among the Somalis.

If I couldn't talk to the girls, I could at least meet the parents in the community. Mohamed Nur, the president of the Somali Community Center of Colorado, agreed to help. His fast-paced enthusiasm, megawatt smile, and knowing voice are a comfort to his people. "We are the only ones who are here for each other," he said. "Do you understand?"

Of course, I understood. I had visited mosques in Virginia with a large Somali congregation and heard their war stories of trauma, torture, and terrible-life incidents. "Because they have seen so much pain, they stay close to each other. They are a tight-knit community that is unbreakable," one Muslim convert told me of the Somalis.

One night, Nur gathered parents from his community in the center to speak to me about their children. I wanted to learn how they were coping with the East African girls' experience with ISIS. How the girls became radicalized is a question that many are still trying to understand, and there is still no adequate answer. Except that it happened online. Behind closed doors, the three girls sat at their laptops, surfing the Internet until an ISIS recruiter found them. What they said, and how they were found, is unclear. My mentor Dr. Post calls this the fifth wave of terrorism: the virtual community of hatred.[3]

Inside the center, families sat on folding chairs around a long table laden with a platter of cookies and plastic cups filled with juice. The women wore colorful hijabs and long skirts. They had a look of uncertainty and curiosity.

"How did your lives change after the girls were found?"

"Every night, I take my teenage daughter's cell phone and check everything," a father in a white dress shirt said, his voice bending like a fallen tree.

The room smelled spicy, strange, and striking. The women were perfumed in a fragrance that was luminous with jasmine-like notes and a bitter earthiness. If I had closed my eyes, I might have thought I'd wandered into an Arab marketplace.

The father continued to talk about the dangers of online recruitment, saying the only way to protect the girls of his community was to "watch over them." I wondered if being under too much parental control and leading isolated lives, with only three places to go— school, the mosque, and their home—compelled the girls to seek freedom online. It made sense to me. I had heard stories of and seen other Muslim girls in ultraconservative households look for friendship and fun to escape their overbearing families. In today's digital age, Muslim girls have access to an entire world online with numerous social media platforms through which to befriend almost anyone, which is exactly what happened. And because the East African girls were technologically savvy, they could easily erase text messages and mask their chats with strangers to keep their parents in the dark. The American poet Robert Frost famously wrote, "Home is the place where, when you have to go there, they have to take you in."[4] Which is exactly what happened with the girls who had joined ISIS: their fathers welcomed them back home, even though it was shameful and an embarrassment to the community.

A woman sitting next to the man, whom I assumed to be his wife, stared with wide eyes and smiled. "We have no choice," she said softly. "If we don't watch our daughters, who will?"

*And what about the boys?* I wondered. There was no mention of teenage boys, who could be just as devious and dangerous. In Minnesota, there have been cases of Somali boys being recruited by a terrorist group in East Africa. But I didn't want to pressure the parents to talk about their sons. I was just glad to listen.

"I have to check who they [the girls] talk to and where they go when they are in school or after school," the father chimed in.

"Really? You don't trust them?"

"Do you trust *your* children?" he asked, leaning forward as his face tightened and he crossed his hands.

"Yes, I guess I do," I said. "Though I have never checked their phones."

"Parents should never trust their children," he replied, coolly. "You can't trust children these days. They don't know what is right or wrong. We have to know what is right. We have to teach them. It's our Muslim duty as parents."

*You're right. I have to tell my teenagers about ISIS, but what will I say?*

"The world is not the same," he concluded.

I had read somewhere that ninety percent of parenting is presence. But I knew I could not overstep cultural boundaries and openly ask the questions that burned inside of me: Why are your girls only allowed in school and at the mosque? What opportunities are you providing to your children? What lessons have you really learned from the girls who joined ISIS, aside from keeping a close watch? And what can you change within yourself to be a better, kinder, and more understanding Muslim parent?

In the Somali community center, I listened to other women sitting around the table. One woman agreed to speak with me privately. We went inside an adjacent room in the back of the center, plastered with vibrant-colored clothing hand-stitched by the local women.

"This is the work we do," she told me. "The women work at home to support the community and feel they are a part of something." The clothing reminded me of handmade shawls and bags I saw in India and Pakistan stitched by poor women to provide for their families.

The woman, whom I will call Sarah, began telling me about the women she trained in their homes, encouraging them to live for themselves and contribute to their families. Most of all, Sarah insisted that mothers like her talk to their daughters, acting as role models and encouraging their girls to participate in activities that would prepare them as leaders. "Our girls need to join after-school organizations and participate in competitions." She was, in a sense, a social-impact crusader who helped women in her community feel good about life by giving them purpose and instilling pride in their work.

Without wasting time, I asked about ISIS, hoping that Sarah would speak openly, as I promised not to record her voice. I had also told myself that I had to be comfortable in not knowing everything; not discovering the intimate details of that day in October when the media revealed the girls' escape and return; and not understanding how long it takes a family, or a community, to heal from an incident like this.

"How did you feel about the Sudanese girl who joined ISIS?"

"This was a shock to all of us. We could have never expected that such a thing would happen here and to us. After it happened, I remember we had a town hall meeting with the Somalis, Sudanese, and other East Africans. We talked about what we needed to do next. We discussed ways to be stronger and more aware. We all agreed we had to find a solution together."

I wanted to know how Sarah, a mother of two girls and a working professional, *felt*. In my travels, I have always found that women have a special place where their emotions are their own. In closed cultures and societies, women often speak freely with other women.

"I know why this happened," she began. "Because we don't give our girls a chance to do anything."

"Do you mean after school?"

"Yes, and in school. After the incident, I let my eldest daughter join a club. She started her own group too. She is happy in school. It is not just a place to study."

"Yes, children need more than their books," I agreed.

"Where is the Sudanese girl now?"

"She's at home." Sarah lowered her voice, and I wanted to understand how a girl who was once radicalized returned to her home as if nothing had happened. The girl who once joined ISIS did not have her life back. Her father likely still felt ashamed for his daughter's actions, even after a year had passed.

"She is not in school like the Somali girls who got on that plane. This girl is isolated. She's alone."

*She probably does not want to be alone*, I thought. *She wants to love and be loved. This could be the most common reason why teenagers and women under the age of thirty join ISIS. Girls need affection and purpose, and as Sarah told me, some girls desire an unfettered life, without cultural and religious controls. It became clear to Sarah that girls need opportunities, too.*

Love is an intoxicating, supreme emotion. In her book *Love 2.0: Finding Happiness and Health in Moments of Connection*, Barbara Fredrickson writes about love as a deeply personal feeling that requires connection. Research by terrorism scholars has shown that many females join violent groups for the sake of love—their relationship to a family member captured or killed in conflict provides an easy pathway for girls and women to enter the extremists' social engagement system. As English poet David Whyte wrote, "There is no house like the house of belonging."[5] The need to belong is exacerbated by the social isolation that Muslim girls and women often feel when their mobility is limited to the home, mosque, and school. Violent extremism is their new tribe, offering females a group to be a part of, a place in the social world where they can feel like they belong. Theirs is an unhealthy group, as they bond together *against* someone or something, a sick substitution for real connection.

"Do you know what the sad thing is?" Sarah said.

I waited for the revelation that would confirm or deny my findings and research. I waited for the words that only a mother determined to save her girls from ISIS could know or say.

"ISIS gives our girls freedom," she said. "Terrorists give our daughters a chance to be someone else and to do something more. We have to do better than that."

It was invigorating to hear a woman who understood the basic needs of Muslim girls—that they are no different from any American teenagers wishing to be free and independent, and wanting to be adults, even when they are still children. Sarah continued to talk about the greater good when girls are empowered—when they are free to move, speak, and just be; when girls who grow up to be women have a choice in marriage—and said that her girls would be encouraged to work outside the home. She spoke of her feeling that marriage is not always at the end of the search for real love. The Holy Grail that parents seek—a relationship that encompasses love, trust, and companionship—could be achieved because this mother believed it possible. Sarah was speaking for all mothers who seek an attachment and understanding with their teenage daughters—to love without judgment and to forgive a child's small and big mistakes. As a mother, I understood how important it is to bond with my teenage daughter and allow her to grow as an American *and* Muslim because the two are not incompatible.

When Sarah left, I tried to unravel the words spoken thus far by community members that played in my mind like pages torn from a journal. I wondered about the synthetic connections we compulsively seek and forge, and the need for completeness. I had been taught, as a Muslim woman, that a community is stronger in numbers. The *Ummah*, or global family, is an extension of the self, and only in our togetherness can Muslims—digitally and otherwise—screen against extremist recruitment and propaganda.

Three Somali males entered the room: a teenager who went to school with the Somali would-be-ISIS girls; his elder brother, Mahad, also a youth leader at the center and a college student; and their friend, a die-hard political activist eager to return to Somalia to become the next president. I introduced myself to them as a Muslim mother, grateful to hear their views as I tried to understand how and why ISIS preyed on girls and boys like them.

"It is easy to join ISIS here," said Mahad in a soft, unconcerned voice.

There was something wrong with the words that came out of his mouth. They were too casual, careless, and informal.

"Why do you say that?" I asked.

"Look around us. We have problems in our community. We have kids who don't know Islam, and their parents don't teach them. So many children are confused."

Misguided, I thought. This was typical of the "cultural" Muslim trend that had existed in America since the arrival of Muslim immigrants, refugees, and asylum seekers. For a while, I had been a "cultured" Muslim girl who migrated to the rolling hills of Tennessee and settled into a small town outside of Nashville, too young to remember the wars my mother experienced or the political turmoil between secularists and Islamists that swept across Pakistan during my parents' time. Unlike Mahad and the boys in front of me, I did not know trauma, abuse, rage, or the wounds of war. I would experience these emotions through the people I interviewed who had experienced protracted conflict.

"What we need is the 'right' Islam," Mahad continued.

For the next hour, we had a frank discussion about what it was like to be a Somali-American Muslim boy. The young men told me stories of their past, a dark period in Somalia when war devastated everything. I could partly relate, as I had witnessed the ugliness of war in faraway places, though I had never suffered its consequences. I listened to stories of hurt. One of the Somalis was recruited into a terrorist group as a boy; he escaped at age fourteen to the largest refugee camp in Kenya, where girls were routinely raped and damaged. He was granted asylum in the United States, only to live in a tightly knit Somali community. These stories were common, and yet I could not begin to imagine the collective visual memories that marked this childhood: forced kidnappings, exposure to violence and death, the onslaught of immigration interviews, and the images of children with guns.

Mahad seemed sure of himself. He showed an ambitious streak as he described his single answer to countering violent extremists.

"Islam is the way," he said, sounding like a preacher. "We need a handbook. I've always thought that we needed a guidebook, like a training manual, to teach young people how to be correct Muslims. That's what they need. They need to know that Islam can uplift you, instead of learning about Islam on the Internet. If we teach Islam the way it should be practiced, then we can save the youth."

I wondered who had taught Mahad the "correct" Islam. Had he learned from his parents? Had he sought a scholar? For many "cultured" Muslims, a series of events that often take place in college and with the influence of mentors allows for an Islamic "awakening"; Muslims like Mahad are then able to shed their cultural identity and embrace Islam's religious unity.

"I had to learn Islam on my own," he said. "When I grew up, I began to see what was happening to the community. Boys dropped out of school for whatever reason and then became addicts. Kids need to be grounded in their faith. When they know what Islam says, they won't be weak."

I reassured the young man that there is a handbook. In fact, there are hundreds of good books on Islam. I told Mahad that he didn't have to look back at the classics; a series of contemporary books on Islam, including concise guides, were readily available. There was no need for funds or time. He just needed his community's support to build awareness among the youth, whom he cared so much about.

"This is my dream," Mahad concluded. "To learn and teach Islam."

His brother, who wished to be unnamed, listened to Mahad admiringly, nodding in agreement.

"After the girls were arrested and came back home, was it easy for them to return to school?" I asked.

"We welcomed them," the teenager said. "Because we have a lot of Somalis at the high school, we stick together. There was no shame in what they did. We knew it could happen to any one of us."

*It could happen to any one of us.* I mulled the words over and over until they made sense to me: the idea that the girl who joined ISIS could be your sister, your friend, or your classmate—anyone who belonged to an inner circle, a tightly knit community that was both familiar and family-friendly, which explains how the Somali sisters made friends again, and their community let go of judgment.

The boy talked about the way the girls had been able to fit in again. They were unafraid and unashamed. Listening to him talk about the girls as his sisters made me aware of what I had learned from other researchers: the in-group dynamics of the Somalis are based on their love and protection for one another, explained in part by their exposure to traumatic events and victimization back home, and the bonding togetherness that comes from knowing they left behind a country ruined by senseless war and raging Muslim fanatics. The once-radicalized Somali girls' private histories had become public knowledge, forcing them out of isolation and back into their normal teenage selves. The scandal they once caused had been forgiven and almost forgotten.

Nevertheless, the powerful familial bonds that existed in the Somali community did not always protect the girls from predators like ISIS. Despite their kinship ties to one another, the three girls found freedom online. Outside of school and the mosque, girls belonging to ultraconservative families were prevented from participating in extracurricular activities at school or elsewhere; they were shamed for talking to boys outside of their faith; and in most cases, they were forbidden to enjoy Western customs and culture. The latter is also true for Muslim children in other ethnic-based communities living in the United States. Thus, Valentines and Halloween were off-limits.

A friend of Mahad's spoke next; his vision for fighting extremism was shaped by his family's political involvement in Somalia's future. "I want to be a great leader," he said with a sense of solemnity, an assuredness that could have been lost in a conversation about vulnerable youth. Moved by a passion to change Somalia, the young man expressed the need to be among his people.

*Then why are you in America?* I thought. I could understand his desire to effect positive change in his birth country, but it still bothered me that America was a temporary place for him until he could pursue his political ambitions.

"I will return one day. You will see me lead my country."

I turned back to Mahad, whose perfect stillness was disquieting. *What are you thinking?* I wondered. I sensed his discomfort the more I probed the thoughts of the troubled youth. I wanted to provide him warmth and energy so that he could fulfill his dream of helping disaffected Somali youth move beyond their larger-than-life tragedies. But I recognized that in the final moment, even as we said "*Salaam*" and walked out together, Mahad regretted speaking openly to me. This was confirmed to me when, weeks later, he turned his phone off and changed his number. He had been told, or so I guessed, to stop talking to anyone for fear of reprisal by the authorities—that his alarming and unpalatable statement, "It is easy to join ISIS here," could prompt an investigation.

Chapter Six

# MISGUIDED

*Arvada, Colorado*

It all seemed innocent enough, until it wasn't. On July 2, 2014, Shannon Maureen Conley was halfway down the runway at Denver International Airport when US federal agents put an end to her plans. Clothed in a hijab, the 19-year-old American girl was on a one-way trip to Turkey via Germany when she was discovered. The Muslim convert made no secret of the fact that she was heading to Syria to join ISIS. A simple-looking American girl, Conley had been radicalized within a short time period. In less than a year, she had converted to Islam, fallen in love with a Muslim man online, and pledged her loyalty to ISIS. She was one of many Western girls who had been misguided by male extremists, a victim of romantic fatalism.

Conley had grown up in Arvada, a quiet suburb of Denver, in a home with a statue of Saint Francis in the garden. Nothing seemed amiss. Her mother, Ana Maria, was a professor at Regis University. Her father, John, worked in the computer industry and taught martial arts on the side. The youngest of four girls, Conley wore shorts and jeans and hats. She was friendly and a bright student at Arvada West High School.

Raised Catholic, Conley converted to Islam. During her junior year of high school, she began wearing long dresses and flowing head scarves. She and a friend were even photographed in the niqab, or face veil, showing only their eyes. Conley peered through the conservative dress with wire-rimmed glasses. Her behavior unnerved some of her classmates, who would find her kneeling three times a day in the school bathroom to pray. Bob Taylor was her neighbor. "When she first moved in," he said, "she seemed normal, wore clothes most kids wear; then she started wearing the long Islamic garb. She would go down the street here to a park and sit on the swing. Swing in the attire for maybe half an hour at a time. I don't know if she was contemplating or meditating."

Conley's behavior grew more alarming. She came to the attention of authorities when she started to stake out a nearby Christian mega-church, Faith Bible Chapel, in the fall of 2013. Like many evangelical churches around the country, Faith Bible Chapel strongly supported the nation of Israel and the Jewish people. Each year, they held an Israel Awareness Day with food, dancing, and exhibits. The sight of a young woman in a Muslim conservative dress, dashing in and out of services and classes, made members uncomfortable. The church had reason to be on edge. In December 2007, a man had opened fire in a missionary group's dormitory housing. Two members died and two others were injured in the senseless crime.

Soon enough, the pastor and the church congregation began to notice that something seemed wrong with Shannon Conley. According to a criminal complaint obtained by the *Denver Post*, Conley said to her religious community, "Why is this church worried about a terrorist attack?" Once, with a pencil and notepad in hand, Conley pretended to draw the layout of the church as she surveilled the place. She told everyone that she was a Muslim doing research. When asked by an Aurora police detective why she was going to the church, Conley replied, "I hate those people. If they think I'm a terrorist, I'll give them something to think I am." Concerned, the church told Conley not to return.

Four days later, the FBI contacted Conley. According to the authorities, extremists were using the Internet to recruit American girls by offering them love and purpose. And this wasn't the first time. Before Conley, I had examined the case of Colleen LaRose, a fifty-year-old woman in Pennsylvania who called herself "Jihad Jane." At the time, the media were fixated on one particular question: Was LaRose acting alone? I remember responding with a flat no.

"Women are lured into terrorist organizations by men. In all my years, I have never seen a woman acting completely alone," I told the press. However, at the time of the breaking story, it was too early to tell what relationship LaRose might have had with other men or women. The press had little to no information about the vast network that was likely in place to draw LaRose into violent extremism.

In 2009, LaRose was arrested for planning to attack Lars Vilks, a Swedish artist who drew offensive cartoons of the Prophet Muhammad, a crime that conservative Muslims punish with death. LaRose was not alone. Like other women and girls who are radicalized, she had a relationship online with an extremist male, who persuaded her to participate in an ultimately failed plot to assassinate Vilks.

The same would be true of Conley. In an early conversation, my journalist friend Vicky Collins described the nineteen-year-old girl as unsure of herself. Conley behaved like a rebel teenager-turned-adult. Like the East African girls, Conley found artificial affection and admiration on the dark web, but this toxic affection was manipulative and short-lived. She found Islam when she met online a Muslim man who convinced the American girl of the righteousness of "holy war" and invited her to join him in service to God. She changed her name from Shannon Conley to Halima, an Arabic name that means "gentle, mild-mannered, and generous."

With a new persona, Conley described herself as a "slave to Allah." Her social media accounts were filled with photos of mosques and quotes from the Quran, and she was intrigued by a British television report about women joining the jihad in Syria. On her Google Plus account, she wrote, "When there are so few mujahideen, is it not our duty to fight regardless of our country of birth and/or residence?" Her Google Plus page also mentioned "The Caravan of Martyrs," a phrase once coined by Osama bin Laden to describe those who gave their lives for jihad. And when al-Qaeda's top spiritual guide, a former American cleric in Virginia, Anwar al-Awlaki, was killed in a US drone strike, Conley said a prayer: "May Allah accept his martyrdom."

What Conley did online was not surprising. Taking on a new faith, she needed acceptance. Many girls her age or younger turn to the online space and social media sites for instant gratification, friendship, and connection, explorations that are not exclusively Muslim. In her book *American Girls: Social Media and the Secret Lives of Teenagers*, Nancy Jo Sales exposes the new coming-of-age practices for girls. They experience first crushes, longing, and romances in an "accelerated electronic environment." Although Sales is referring to non-Muslims, the same is true for Muslim girls and converts developing affairs online with Muslim men they hardly know because it feels safe and "Islamic." For girls like Conley, the social media world is explosive, offering a wide medium of new communication platforms such as Ask.fm, Kik, Tinder, DM, and so many more. To the youth, the technology is easy, fast, and private—most parents, who did not grow up in the digital age, simply don't know how to access or use the Internet.

Conley's online love affair with an ISIS recruiter was partially to blame for poisoning her with toxic rhetoric. His real name was Yousr Mouelhi (YM). Conley called the thirty-two-year-old Tunisian man who fought for ISIS her "suitor." She made plans to fly out of Denver International Airport on a United Airlines flight for Frankfurt, Germany, on April 8, 2014; take a Lufthansa flight to Istanbul; and then board a Turkish airliner to Adana, Turkey, where she would drive with her handler-cum-lover to the Syrian-Turkish border and begin a new life in Syria as a housewife and a camp nurse, which made sense since she had worked as a certified nurse's aide in Colorado. Conley also said that she wished to fight a guerrilla war in the Middle East or work as a nurse.[1]

Before she could leave for Syria, Conley was told she had to marry Mouelhi. Under Islamic law, a woman needs two witnesses and the permission of a male guardian. In Conley's case, her male guardian was her father, John; he knew that his daughter was talking to a foreign Muslim man and attempted to interrupt the Skype conversations that his daughter was having with her lover-handler, YM. After YM proposed over Skype, Conley asked her father for his blessing to marry him. John said no.

His refusal made no difference.

When John found his daughter's one-way ticket to Turkey, he notified the FBI, and her arrest was set in motion. In a similar fashion, the father of the Sudanese girl also helped the authorities to locate the girls and return them to their homes in Aurora. But Conley, given her age and multiple exchanges with FBI agents, would not go home.

Conley's use of the Internet to "find" Islam is an all-too-familiar story. Instead of turning to a scholar or the mosque community, Conley used Google and found a plethora of articles and videos by self-professed scholars using the Internet to teach a perverted Islam. According to Conley's arrest affidavit, "She conceded her knowledge of Islam was based solely on her own research that she conducted on the Internet."

Before Conley's arrest, local authorities had been watching. Between November 2013 and April 2014, federal agents called Conley in for questioning eight times. She had no misgivings about her plans. She told the agents that her weekend of military-style training would come in handy in a holy war. She received training at Young Explorers, an organization loosely affiliated with the US Army and the Boys Scouts of America, which Conley said would be useful when she was "to go overseas to wage jihad . . . and [pursue] legitimate targets of attack," which included US military facilities, government employees, and public officials. She proclaimed that "it is acceptable to attack Westerners . . . in defense of jihad." The agents asked Conley what she would do if innocents were harmed in the process of jihad. According to court documents, Conley said that if wives, children, and chaplains had the bad luck to be killed during an attack on a military base, so be it. They should not have been there in the first place. It seemed that collateral damage was inevitable.

If her candor was jaw-dropping to the agents, they didn't show it. Looking back, it's surprising how patient and understanding the authorities had been with Conley as they tried to persuade her to pursue progressive Islam and use her new religion to do good, humanitarian work. Authorities warned her repeatedly that her thoughts and actions could get her into trouble.

In an attempt to intervene, the agents asked Conley's parents to help steer her toward more moderate mentors, but the ardent supporter of ISIS could not be dissuaded. She was determined, she told the FBI, to be "defending Muslims on the Muslim homeland against people who are trying to kill them . . . jihad is the only answer to correct the wrongs against the Muslim world." When asked if she would engage in combat, Conley told authorities that it was the duty of men to fight, but "if it was absolutely necessary, then yes."

Looking at her past and family life, can we explain Conley's turning to Islam as she vocally denounced the Faith Bible Church? Can we understand the longing of an American girl whose need for affection and belonging led her into the fold of ISIS? Can we identify early problems that Conley may have exhibited, such as low self-esteem, anxiety, depression, relationship and family issues, difficulty at school, trouble with her faith, and questions about her identity? As with other women I have studied or spoken with, Conley's desire to learn about Islam and eventually join ISIS was personal—she found her identity, belonging, and meaning through violent extremism.

To be fair, Conley's parents tried to talk to their daughter about her online activities. According to John, Conley used her own laptop and refused to show her parents whom she was talking to and what she intended to do. All they knew was that their daughter had changed her name and accepted a new religion, of which they knew little about. John also knew that Conley was chatting with YM, a man she wanted to marry overseas and migrate to Syria with. Conley told her father that she wanted to marry a "soldier" and that if she could not fight, "she [would] still be supporting his cause."

In 2014, on several occasions, John and his wife, Ana, tried to engage Conley in candid conversation about their daughter's views on Islam. In March 2014, John called Special Agent (SA) Matthew J. Dahl and reported Shannon's religious beliefs. "Conley explained to her father she felt conflicted with what she thought Islam required of her" and believed that a Muslim girl needed to marry young and be "confrontational in her support of Islam," according to a US District Court criminal complaint report.[2] Conley also admitted to her father that her knowledge of Islam was based on her own research that she conducted on the Internet.[3]

Six days before Conley was going to head to Turkey, John reported to SA Dahl that he and his wife did not support their daughter's marriage to an ISIS recruiter. But it was too late. Conley was convinced that being a good Muslim woman meant she had to marry into ISIS for the same reasons that other girls her age joined the group—to support a Caliphate and its men. No matter how they tried to dissuade their daughter, neither John nor Ana could stop their daughter from leaving for Syria.

On January 23, 2015, Conley appeared in court in hijab and a striped, blue-and-white prison jumpsuit. US District Judge Raymond Moore charged Conley with providing material support to a terrorist group; it carried a fifteen-year prison sentence. For the next hour, an intense back and forth between Judge Moore; Assistant US Attorney Gregory Holloway; and Conley's attorney, public defender Robert Pepin, made it difficult to know which way the judge would lean with his sentence. Pepin wanted Conley's sentence reduced to forty-eight months. Holloway demanded a longer jail time to send a message and discourage other young Americans from joining terrorist groups, online or offline. The assistant US attorney insisted to the court that Conley had to be the first and last extremist in the state.

Luckily for Conley, the judge allowed her testimony saying that she had no intentions of hurting anyone. Conley had no criminal history; Holloway reminded the court that Hayat Boumeddiene, a twenty-six-year-old woman wanted by French police in connection with several terror attacks in Paris in early 2015 at the time of the Charlie Hebdo massacre, who fled to Syria, also had no prior criminal history. The prosecutor suggested that leniency would send the wrong message to other would-be extremists like Conley and therefore insisted that the court punish her for her intention to plan a terrorist attack, for which there was no "hard" evidence of terrorist plotting.

Pepin mounted a strong defense. He told the court that Conley had suffered enough after spending almost a year in jail. She had lost her dream of being a certified nursing assistant and needed mental health care rather than a trip to prison. He also swore that Conley had changed her mind about violent jihad: she changed her name from Halima to Amatullah, "servant of God."

But the judge was not impressed. "Don't tell me that changing her name means she gets it. She changes her name like I change my socks," he said. However, the defense argued that Conley deserved the right to integrate back into her home and society. "We've had enough swords," Pepin said.

In the late afternoon, Conley was invited to speak. She faced the judge with the look of a woman beaten down. She admitted her guilt, her face marked with regret for joining ISIS. She cried while reading a written statement: "Even though I supported a jihad, it was never to hurt anyone. It was always in the defense of Muslims. . . . I do not believe I am a threat to society, and I hope you give me a chance to prove it."[4] Her emotions overpowered her; at one point, she had to sit down to compose herself. "I disavow these radical views," she said, as she pleaded for mercy.

Conley told the court she was a changed woman. "I am sincerely grateful to the FBI for preventing me from going to Syria," she said, because it had saved her life. She said she read the Quran with an open mind and understood that the people she met online had distorted Islam. But she had discovered the "true" Islam, a religion of peace.[5]

Conley asked the judge to grant her a new life. "This has been a life-altering experience," she said, and she was ready to be a "catalyst for good." Conley concluded her statement by telling the court that she was not the same person. She said she had changed after spending some time alone in prison: "I started my incarceration hateful. I have grown. I do not believe I am a threat to society and would appreciate the chance to prove it. I ask you to let me move forward and begin a positive chapter of my life."[6]

I wish Conley would have been pardoned—forgiven because she had repented and realized her wrongs, and because she promised to correct her behavior. I wished for Judge Moore to be merciful to this new Muslim believer whose confusion and carelessness was a reflection of something deeper than a superficial desire to "be" Muslim. I had seen other American men and women come to Islam—each wanting to belong, to fill a void, a lingering emptiness that existed in their lives, and to find meaning in an existence bruised by past and present difficulties. A straggling few leave America for "a Muslim country"—a concept that I have argued does not exist. No country in the world as we know it is as compassionate and forgiving to its people as the Prophet of Islam was to the early followers.

In his closing remarks, Judge Moore acknowledged to the court that this was not an easy case, and he believed there were mental health issues that needed to be addressed. He recognized that Conley had no age-appropriate friendships—that she was isolated, young, naïve, and uncomfortable with herself. Then he began to scold her.

"You can't moonwalk back from your admissions," he said. "The public interest factors cut against you." Judge Moore also questioned Conley's "changed" self. He said, "I'm still not sure what's been crystallized in your mind." He reminded Conley that this was a very serious offense, a crime punishable by fifteen years of imprisonment and a lifetime of supervised release. But because of her cooperation with federal authorities, he said, Conley deserved a lesser sentence.

After his statement, the judge announced his decision. Conley received the minimum four years, or forty-eight months, with three years of supervised release, followed by one hundred hours of community service. He also waived the $250,000 fine.

For the next four years of her life, Conley would serve her sentence in federal prison in Golden, Colorado, a breathtaking city with miles of green hills along Clear Creek that lies at the base of the Rocky Mountains. The judge made it clear that Conley was to have no more communication with ISIS or al-Qaeda.

I remember feeling relieved that Conley had another opportunity at life. Perhaps in prison, she might study scripture and one day find a Muslim community in Denver to help her see what I have always known: that Islam is a religion of peace, mercy, and compassion; and the Islam preached and practiced by violent extremists is a distortion and a disgrace of the ancient religion.

In January 2015, Conley's parents released a statement to the press. For the first time since their daughter's hearing, John and Ana, who have now since separated, sent a letter to President Obama and the American people, hoping that the country would see Conley as an innocent victim of violent extremists:

### An Open Letter to the President and the American People

*Over the last several months my wife and I have received numerous requests for a statement about our daughter Shannon's situation. Now that she has been sentenced we would offer these thoughts.*

*We were told at the time of the investigation the Department of Justice (FBI and Federal Prosecutor's Office) was trying to formulate a better response to young people being radicalized by ISIS and other groups. In doing so the local personnel went to extraordinary lengths to navigate the turbulent waters caused by these events. In our dealings with them we have been treated with respect and compassion throughout this affair. It's unfortunate the local efforts apparently weren't viewed as more worthwhile by their superiors.*

*The strategy of the terrorist is to make the enemy change behavior through the use of fear and to subjugate the enemy by making them live in fear. A tactic of asymmetric warfare is to cause the enemy to expend large amounts of resources dealing with a situation that costs little to create. . . .*

*We're told the government is afraid that, even if Shannon is not a threat to the public, others may make similar choices. Those people need to be sent a message that if they do they should fear capture and prosecution. Shannon's continued punishment is to ensure that message is understood by the American people. Additionally the, perhaps unintended, message is the government is willing to sacrifice the future of a 19 year old American citizen to drive the point home. . . .*

*Everyone that has been directly involved with the case has told us they do NOT view Shannon as a threat to the public and that she isn't a "terrorist." They tell us that she was an incredibly naïve and idealistic young woman who trusted that others were telling her the truth about things happening in a distant land. This led her to make bad choices for which she continues to pay a very high price.*

*Almost all of ISIS' barbaric actions were reported after Shannon's arrest. She is appalled by them and realizes ISIS is trying to cover up their savagery with a religious veil which cannot be justified within the teachings of Islam. She acknowledges her poor judgment and is struggling to discover how she will be able to put her life back together as a "felon." Thus, she also is not a flight risk.*

*We have been saddened not only by how the media has tried to sensationalize this situation but how quickly many have been willing to condemn our daughter without even reading the public legal record, much less having direct knowledge of the facts in her case or the law surrounding it. We know a very different person from the one that's been portrayed in the "news" reports and have had our view of her confirmed over and over by others who have met her for the first time during the course of this ordeal.*

*The conditions that led to Shannon's (and others') choices to try to go to the Middle East are complex and we have no easy answers to address them. We certainly have no "sound bites" to offer on how to win the War on Terrorism. We do feel that a step in the right direction is to not give into fear. This choice bears a risk but taking that risk is a behavior America was built upon and, in our view, is worth taking.*

The stories I found in Denver reinforced for me how vulnerable are girls and young women to being recruited by ISIS. The East African community had left indelible imprints on me. There were the girls outside the local mosque with knowing eyes, who I believed had so much to say but were afraid to speak in front of adults. The Sudanese mother who dared to speak the truth and took steps to empower her own girls was an inspiration. Most of all, I am grateful to the East African women who allowed me to see that I had an obligation to speak to my teenagers about terrorism.

Until that point, my only concern had been dropping my kids off at school, cooking for them, washing and folding their clothes, helping with homework, and answering their off-the-wall questions: Why do some Muslims hate dogs? Who is a Shia? Why do I have to read the Quran when I don't understand it? Are we orthodox? Do I have to go to Sunday school?

A visit with the Somalis made me painfully aware of the times we live in. When I arrived home, I had "the" talk.

"I need to talk to you," I said to my son and daughter.

"Did we do something wrong?" my son asked.

"Are we going to meditate together? Because I don't have time today," my daughter said, disgruntled.

"This is more serious than you think. Sit down, please."

With bewildered eyes, they sat across from each other, holding on to their iPhones.

"Give me your phones."

"I only play games," the boy said.

"I need to read your text messages."

"I'm going to delete my history before I give it to you," they agreed.

*Why would you do that? Your father can hack into any system. He's an IT guru, if you hadn't noticed*, I thought.

"You can't do this to us!" the girl exclaimed.

"Do you know your religion?" I asked. It was a simple question. An ordinary question about knowing right from wrong, respecting others, choosing love over hate, and being strong and disciplined enough to say no to drugs, sexual predators, and terrorists.

"Tell me," I said, "what does Islam mean to you?" I wanted to know.

"Are you going to spy on us?"

"Not yet," I said. We all laughed.

"What *is* Islam?" I waited for an answer.

"It's one of those questions that you don't know how to answer but you know the answer," the youngest responded as her brother leaned back into the chair, laughing.

*I have to make them understand. I can't let my children be blinded by the fake Muslims of the world.*

"Extremists are a threat," I began. "They are very smart. They will talk to you on Facebook and Twitter. They know how to DM you. They will try to be your friend. They will tell you what Islam is and what you need to do to be a better Muslim. They will tell you to hate everything that is here. You cannot listen to *anyone* on the Internet about Islam. Not even people you think you know. No Muslim online is better than a Muslim offline. Do you understand what I'm saying?"

"OK, we get it. Can we go now? I have homework," my daughter said.

Conversations with the mothers of Colorado helped me understand the challenges of talking to children about a threat they could not yet perceive or did not believe was real. Parents understood that the threat to their community was real: their children could easily fall prey to ISIS after viewing hours of extremist propaganda behind closed doors, especially at home, increasing their chances of being radicalized. At the "Google Ideas" conference in Dublin, Ireland, in 2011, participants examined the role of the Internet—specifically chat rooms, video posts, and social networking—to explain recruitment to extremist groups. One of the attendees was a former radical from Canada, Mubin Shaikh, coauthor of *Undercover Jihadi: Inside the Toronto 18—Al Qaeda Inspired, Homegrown Terrorism in the West*. On several occasions, I have listened to Shaikh tell his personal story about becoming a radical and then turning away from radical Islam with the help of a saint-scholar in Syria.

The father of four children, Shaikh alludes to the "nature versus nurture" argument: the influence of one's physical environment, upbringing, family, and value systems. After twenty years of research on radicalization, Shaikh reaffirms what I have known to be true: it's a process triggered by an individual's conflict over meaning and identity. In his book and lectures, Shaikh describes his dual life: at the madrasa, where he learned a harsh-rules-only Islam, and at public school, which gave him freedom and friendship without judgment. "This laid the foundation of an identity crisis," he explained once. To a lesser extent, I experienced the duality of growing up Muslim in Texas, often mistaken for Mexican-American, ignorant of Islamic history and principles; and like Shaikh, I found school to be a nurturing place.

Years later, when he traveled to Syria, Shaikh rediscovered the depth of the Quran by training under a Sufi saint. "I learned that jihad is not fighting, but that there's a different word for this, which is *qital*," he told me. This was the first time Shaikh realized that saving the Muslim world by violent jihad is not rooted in Islam—the blame belongs to radical groups who misinterpret and misuse the faith for personal and political gain. "In Syria, I had a theological framing," Shaikh said. "I learned the Quran. I learned what the verses of the holy book meant. For example, the Quran uses the word 'the polytheists' to refer to a very specific group of people at a specific time; it does not refer to the Jews and Christians, who are the People of the Book."

Returning to Canada, Shaikh described his journey back into Islam as an undercover agent for the Canadian intelligence service. He wanted to save his community from radicalizing. On his own time, Shaikh trolled the Internet helping to keep the Muslim youth, including girls, from being recruited by ISIS. If watching extremist videos for a prolonged period places an individual at severe risk of recruitment, then de-radicalization can take an equal amount of time and effort to save a potential recruit. The work takes hours of discussing the peaceful practice of Islam with Muslims looking for meaning, belonging, and identity. Sometimes, it can take up to a year.

Meeting Shaikh helped me understand how important it is to stay engaged with children at home. Keeping an eye on their online and offline activities allows parents to know they are safe from bullies, sexual predators, and extremists like ISIS. I thought about all the mothers who had lost their children to radical Islam and didn't know it. There are numerous cases of mothers in European cities whose sons ran away from home to join ISIS. Sadly, the families did not notice the change in their children because "they just couldn't perceive it. It was not until the sons were gone, only then they realized how they were changing. . . . They were just sort of radicalizing slowly, and a lot of the women just couldn't understand that at that time," said photographer-journalist Poulomi Basu, who interviewed three mothers whose children joined ISIS from the ethnically diverse town of Vilvoorde outside of Brussels.[7]

I attended meetings of a family-life initiative, created to address the needs of Muslim parents in America, held on Sundays at the Fawakih Manor in Herndon, Virginia. Beginning in April 2016, the six-week program used a business model to help Muslim families understand their role as parents, their relationship with the community, and their connection with God. With Imam Mohamed Magid, a Somali leader at the ADAMS center, the course was designed to strengthen the Muslim family with knowledge-based solutions. In groups, I listened to young and older parents express their views: there were few role models, information on Islam was event-driven, learning was an eternal exercise, and communication was essential. I had to believe that consistent and compassionate conversations with my children would help them practice true Islam and steer them away from anything extreme.

As a mother, I learned the important lesson of empowering children with the right information. Intervention has to start early and be consistent. With two teenagers, I know the limits of their hearing and the effect of short attention spans. In speaking with other Muslim parents, I understand that certain words must be repeated at random times to make the message feel continuous and livable: *Islam is a religion of peace, compassion, and mercy* had to be felt and heard like a steady womb-beat. I had to apply models that I use in my counterterrorism work to make it relevant at home: Educate. Engage. Empower.

First, I believe that Muslim children need daily affirmations and parental love. In Proust's *Remembrance of Things Past*, a child waits in bed for his mother to give him a goodnight kiss. In the story, the child becomes isolated and separated from his mother, with whom he longs to reunite. In Plato's version of love, lovers are incomplete until found. In the same way, educating children about Islam involves focusing on God's love for His creation, reminding the youth that the first oral tradition recorded by the Prophet of Islam had to do with God's mercy, and the last sermon by the Prophet to his tribe emphasized equality and inclusion.

Second, Muslim parents can do more to engage their children: discuss real, taboo topics like sex, drugs, and ISIS. And they should encourage children to ask questions about Islam, which most Muslim cultures and countries forbid. Over the years, I have had to respond to the most mundane and surprising questions about Islam. A question is an insight into a child's mind, and even when I don't have the answer, I seek religious guidance and turn to my mentors, who are as transparent as water. They let the light of wisdom flow through them.

Third, identity crises and a feeling of perceived isolation explain why some children become radicalized. Numerous case studies, including the ones in this book, reveal a lack of belonging and a clash of cultures that the youth may feel when they are disempowered at home, ignorant of Islam, and/or compelled to reject mainstream values and the society in which they live. Paradoxically, it is in that moment of alienation that some are open to life, even when it is the wrong kind of empowerment that extremists allegedly promise—an eternal Paradise that they sell to win support.

Rather than restricting behavior and imposing rigid rules, Muslim parents in the West can offer opportunities for their children to spend time with non-Muslim friends, allowing them to form strong attachments with people of other faiths. Growing up, I observed my parents' love for people of other religious traditions. My parents' closest friends were Jewish, Christian, and Hindu, as well as other Muslims in their community. Before I had any Muslim friends, I had surrounded myself with classmates from different cultures and backgrounds.

Finally, as a mother, I have learned how important it is to stay in touch with a child's everyday events and emotions. Child psychologists affirm that understanding your children is the most important thing parents should learn how to do: look for consistent traits; help them develop their self-esteem and social skills, according to the Child Development Institute. Raising balanced children also means less screen time. In her book *Reset Your Child's Brain: A Four-Week Plan to End Meltdowns, Raise Grades, and Boost Social Skills by Reversing the Effects of Electronic Screen Time*, child psychiatrist Victoria L. Dunckley, MD, describes a study she conducted with a group of five hundred children and adolescents.[8] Her work confirms that screen time acts as a psycho-stimulant similar to caffeine and drugs like cocaine: excessive time online also overstimulates the nervous system and leads to a host of issues, from mood swings to concentration problems.

When their children are using the Internet, parents can feel clueless about what material they are reading, which websites they are visiting, and whom they are chatting with. Internet safety expert Nancy Willard offers parents practical strategies in her book *Cyber-Safe Kids, Cyber-Savvy Teens: Helping Young People Learn to Use the Internet Safely and Responsibly*.[9] Even with limited technical knowledge, parents can use the same teaching tools they once applied to younger children with their teenagers to help them make better choices online. Ultimately, experts and psychologists agree that remaining engaged with children is more valuable than using hacking or blocking software.

In today's increasingly digital world, parents have the additional burden of monitoring their children's online activities, such as their tweets, Facebook posts, and Snapchat messages, as well as becoming familiar with their offline friends. As a mother, I am duty-bound to raise loving, caring, and giving children. I hope that they will learn to love everyone and forgive me when I make mistakes. I have a responsibility to teach them that having a balanced life means embracing the beauty of the West while accepting the richness of Islamic history, culture, and civilization, and I pray that I will have the wisdom to know when to let them go.

Chapter Seven

# LOVE OF GOD

*East London*

We wandered together under moody gray skies, stepping into the Turkish neighborhood in East London. The smell of sugar and stale coffee permeated the air. Carrying a tote bag, her hair pulled back in a scarf, a thirty-something woman named Zufie guided me inside an ethnic restaurant with cushions on the floor and lanterns from an imperial era hanging above us. Earlier, we had prayed together at the Turkish mosque nearby, our heads bowed on an ocher-red rug, the walls decorated with bright teal-green leaves, reminding me of the interior of Istanbul's famous Blue Mosque.

If there was a voice that did not need words, it was hers. In the 1990s, when I first met Zufie, I was enrolled in classes at a local university near Hyde Park and lived on Coventry Street. My classes included British Theater and Introduction to the Bible, taught by a priest. When we met, I recognized our differences to be a gift, rather than a barrier to friendship. In time, we made promises to travel together and to honor our new togetherness without judgment, no matter where we might go. Hers was a different world from my American Southern life. She found calm in the midst of bigotry, shadows of doubt, and shame from unwarranted attacks on Islam. But her calming presence and mindful living—originating from her love of God and His creation—helped Zufie discover Islam with grace, leaving no room for hostility or cold-heartedness for those who either demonized her faith or indulged in religious extremism.

At that time, Zufie was an energetic young woman searching for her purpose. London's Muslim population was already burgeoning; many minarets lit up the night sky. Zufie's journey into Islam had been peaceful, without the conflicts that some girls experienced when they shed their home life of secularism and replaced it with radical Islam. Luckily, Zufie discovered "true" Islam from a scholar named Shaykh Nuh, originally based in Jordan, whose focus is on cleansing the soul and living with your whole heart.

London's Muslim community is diverse and distinctive. Because Muslims originate from different countries, the community is increasingly fractured along ethnic, linguistic, and ideological lines. Many mosques have been split by sects of Islam, allowing a culture of intolerance and indifference to enter mainstream society. Some experts have told me that tolerance of alternative lifestyles and views in the UK may have been the perfect breeding ground for radical Islam. In the past, radical imams, facilitators, and planners have used this modern cosmopolitan city as a sanctuary to publicly express hard-line views, support religious extremist groups, and plan deadly attacks such as the 7/7 bombings.

Previously, it was north London that had stronger links to radical Islam. The imam of the Finsbury Park Mosque there, Egyptian cleric Abu Hamza al-Masri, was extradited by the High Court in London to the United States to face trial. In May 2014, a federal jury in New York convicted the fifty-six-year-old cleric on twelve criminal counts, including aiding kidnappers during a 1988 hostage-taking in Yemen and attempting to establish an al-Qaeda–style training camp on the West Coast of the United States. Like Al-Masri, other radicals had once passed through the Finsbury Park Mosque, including the shoe-bomber Richard Reid and Zacarias Moussaoui, who was an accomplice in the 9/11 attacks in the United States.

During my previous trips, I had avoided the Finsbury Park Mosque. However, on Fridays, Zufie escorted me to the palatial mosque in Regent's Park in central London, with its grand chandelier and open spaces. One time, we prayed in the East London Mosque on Whitechapel Road, the oldest mosque in London, with a large community from Bangladesh. The women's upstairs prayer hall was a tight space, overflowing with worshippers, their flat-heeled shoes falling onto the staircase.

Each time I saw Zufie, she had become more serene, more enlightened, and more introspective. Her love of God intensified when she had learned to accept an ancient truth: the war between good and evil is always present. "We live in a world where the war between truth and falsehood is alive," she said. *Yes, the battle between justice and injustice is an old story reenacted in the civil wars of our time*, I thought. Within the good-versus-bad struggle is sacrifice and service to the larger society, which, strangely enough, is what religious radicals believe when they call Muslims to join their reconstruction of Islam, using the Internet as their primary tool to make contact with the youth and convince children that the "Caliphate movement" is their real purpose in life.

Anthropologist Joseph Campbell in *The Power of Myth* distinguishes between the search for meaning and the experience of meaning: "We're so engaged in doing things to achieve purposes of outer value that we forget that the inner value, the rapture that is associated with being alive, is what it's all about."[1] This is why myths and rituals are essential to a healthy society. However, the myths and rituals propagated by religious extremists negate the original principles of Islam. Extremists focus on rituals, such as prayer and fasting, with little understanding of charity, one of the five pillars of Islam and a concept highlighted numerous times in the Quran. Their obedience to God translates into trivialities, such as a strict dress code and a swath of senseless acts. This type of propaganda profoundly affects a child's psychological and emotional well-being.

As more children join ISIS and other groups, counterterrorism experts worry that one of the greatest challenges is that officials may lack the legal authority to track children the same way as they monitor adults. In Europe, children are protected by domestic laws and a commonly held assumption that when young people do bad things, they're going through a phase of adolescence. "They will grow out of it" is often the way misbehavior is excused. Consequently, too often, parents, teachers, religious leaders, and community members don't know what their children are doing.

Zufie pinned this problem on radical Muslim men trolling the Internet for vulnerable women and girls to recruit. She told me, "It's the men who are looking for girls in the chat rooms. Online interaction is a real danger for a child who is thirteen or fourteen and doesn't know any better. A child at that age doesn't always know how to communicate in person or online."

She continued, "The girls of ISIS are confused. They are lost in an online world that is more real to them than the world of their school or family, and it's only getting worse when British Muslims don't know where they come from. Some don't know who or where to belong to, and this affects their self-esteem. These kids have no real understanding of faith or respect for the stories from the past that teach us how to live a balanced and compassionate life. Like the prostitute that God forgave because she saved the dog from dying of thirst—these stories should be passed down to children by their parents or a religious guide." This simple story made me understand the value of a good deed, no matter how small, as well as God's infinite mercy for *everyone*. Charity is the one thing that will save your soul, Mama said.

For many Muslims living in Western countries, these stories are untold, unknown, and thus unfamiliar to the youth. This ignorance of faith, coupled with a host of other societal and familial challenges, contributes to extremist behavior and easy recruitment. In today's digital age, when children and parents lead busier-than-ever lives, the stories of old are never shared, and the books that convey moral lessons from God's messengers are seldom read. Many Muslim children will never experience the spark that occurs during a teaching moment when the past becomes an indelible memory.

Through storytelling that focuses on the life of the Prophet and his companions, Muslim children are given an opportunity to appreciate where they come from. They're able to digest current world events in order to fully understand their surroundings. From the perspective of Islam, they can participate in conversations about challenges of the Muslim youth living in the West.

In lectures I have given on religion, I often allude to the importance of history. If, in fact, the past informs the present and can guide the future, Muslims need to know their scripture. When my children were younger, I read *Goodnight Stories from the Quran*, which begins with God's creation of all things. "He just said the words and there was the earth and the sky. There was the bright sun, the shining moon and twinkling stars. Then came the dry land and the oceans. By just saying the words He made them all . . . thank You, Allah, for making such a wonderful world."[2] The book of stories also includes a tribe called the Children of Israel in Egypt, governed by a cruel pharaoh, who is saved by a beautiful boy named Musa, the Arabic name for Moses.

Knowing these stories reminds children of the value of life. They are inspired to emulate God's attributes: to practice mercy, compassion, tolerance, patience, humility, generosity, awareness, and peace. Many Muslim scholars believe that empowering the youth with the right resources for spiritual growth contributes to civic involvement, a consciousness and acceptance of the society they live in, and the independence to ask *any* question regarding faith from respected online and other sources.

In the early 1940s, the seminal psychologist Abraham Maslow identified "self-actualization" to be an important marker for personal growth: life is believed to be more joyful than painful, and when problems arise, instead of complaining or seeking destructive alternatives, children focus on solutions. Although Maslow did not reference religion or offer a faith-based guide, the highest level of his steps to inner peace is transcendence—for example, when an individual joins a cause beyond him- or herself. This logic appealed to some Muslim women and girls who joined ISIS and expressed their desire to join the group to save lives in order to restore the dignity of Syrian women and children and save them from despair and destruction by rebuilding the war-torn country.

After all, the girls believed, doesn't Islam call Muslims to help those in need? They referenced verses from the Quran—"Surely Allah enjoins justice and the doing of good" (16:90)—without fully understanding the meaning of "doing good" or the concept of justice. These girls, and their spiteful recruiters, forgot that there is nothing Allah hates more than injustice and transgression. In a well-accepted oral tradition, God told his servants, "I have forbidden oppression for Myself and have made it forbidden amongst you. So do not oppress one another."

Zufie and I found a quiet restaurant and settled into our cushions. The air was filled with the scents of garlic, onion, and spices. We shared a plate of grilled kebabs, fries, a Greek salad, and several rounds of coffee. Inside, away from the bitterness of London's winter, I felt warm again. We engaged in conversation about Islam, belonging, and love. I sensed what I had always known about Zufie: her remarkable ability to show mercy for the hateful.

*Love is the eye of awareness*, I said to myself.

In her redemptive voice, Zufie explained, "I have a lot of love for the British, but there are intolerant people even here. This ignorance turns to hate, and it's a constant challenge. The other day, I was on a bus reading the *Guardian* and girls kept teasing me about my headscarf, but it wasn't worth the trouble for me to talk back to them.

"Every year, I attend this huge Islamic conference with Shaykh Nuh," Zufie continued. "When I'm there, there are no labels, no sects, and no names of any kind. We are just Muslims who come together to focus on gaining and passing down knowledge. I go to renew my connection to God and remind myself that Islam is a balanced religion. It's not what other people, including the extremists, make it out to be. All I know is that I belong here."

The need to belong, or not belong, is what drives girls (and boys) toward an idea, person, group, and/or movement that boosts confidence, encourages participation, and promises "Paradise," an expression of eternal happiness that is used literally or figuratively.

Child psychologist Karyn Hall, author of *The Power of Validation: Arming Your Child Against Bullying, Peer Pressure, Addiction, Self-Harm, and Out-of-Control Emotions*, claims that the idea of belonging can be used by those who exclude others to manipulate people. This is the behavior of religious extremists, who isolate themselves from those who reject their worldview and practice of Islam. Their exclusive-members-only idea of belonging can undermine self-control and well-being; often, it leads to pain and conflict.

When I was a student of Dr. Post's in graduate school, I learned that an individual wishing to belong to a terrorist group accepted a "collective identity," and therefore his or her needs and desires ceased to matter. According to Dr. Post, patterns of psychological disorders could explain seeking belonging by joining religious extremism. In the study of individual psychopathology, a person exhibiting patterns of abnormal behavior could be reflective of culture, and what is abnormal in one culture may not be abnormal in another culture. For example, for girls in many Muslim households, befriending boys is forbidden. In a simple expression of love, Mama told me on the way to school, "Don't talk to boys." I had to kindly remind my mother that I had to speak to them to complete projects and school papers. These days, Muslim girls can easily bypass the don't-talk-to-boys rule by using online apps such as Kik or Snapchat. *No parents allowed.*

Zufie was born in London and has always lived on the East End. She was a schoolteacher at Langdon Park, and her students were mostly Muslim and from various ethnic backgrounds. After the 7/7 attacks, teachers like Zufie were asked to look for signs of radicalization inside the classroom: anti-Western, anti-Semitic, or pro-ISIS comments; signs of dramatic change; grades dropping; psychological or emotional signals, such as fear, depression, anxiety, insecurity, avoidance, defensive behavior, disrespect, or hostility. "Kids will be kids," Zufie told me. "We all know that children often mess up. Even a student with good grades can get pregnant. So some level of stupidity is expected." For over a decade, Zufie spent her life at the school, teaching English to Muslim children ages twelve to sixteen. The three girls who escaped to Syria in 2015 were within the age range of students whom Zufie devoted herself to teaching how to be both British and Muslim.

In February 2015, Shamima Begum, Amira Abase, and Kadiza Sultana, from East London, each spent $1,500 to fly to Turkey, where an ISIS handler led them into Syria. The youngest of the three, Begum assumed the identity of her seventeen-year-old sister, Aklima, to travel. When leaving home, the girls told their mothers that they would be late from school; it was the middle of the semester at the school they attended, and it would have been logical for the girls to stay after school for extra tutoring. This was the last time the families would see their girls.

On video camera footage, the British girls, one of them sixteen years old and the other two fifteen years old, looked like ordinary passengers. They sported Western clothes, wearing parkas and shawls, and carried duffle bags, large purses, and backpacks as they walked through the terminal at Gatwick Airport. Video cameras showed them entering the Istanbul airport before they headed for Syria. They never returned. By July, five months later, at least two of the girls married older men in their twenties, one of whom was a Canadian national, chosen for them by other ISIS commanders. In January 2016, the news reported that two of the British Muslim girls were widowed when their husbands died fighting, thus ending the fantasy of happily ever after. (More on the girls in chapter 8.)

"The girls we see joining ISIS are uneducated in Islam," Zufie pointed out. "They don't love God the way God needs to be loved. But how can they know what love is? You need a teacher who has knowledge of the Quran and the *sunnah* [traditions] and someone who is fluent in classical Arabic. These girls don't even know who they are following or who is guiding them. Their ignorance creates lies about our faith, and it's damaging. They need to discipline their soul and find a connection to God. If you are connected to the Creator, who is most merciful, then how can you kill another person? That is contradictory to Islam."

Zufie had once told me that love comes in many forms—passionate love, motherly love, the love of friendship, the love of children or animals—but that the love of God helped her cultivate gratitude and compassion. "We need to know the difference between a sound and balanced Islam versus Islam at face value, which comes from a superficial reading of the Quran," she said.

I had heard this idea before, that true Islam is more than a book. It is a process of soul-searching that nurtures the body, mind, and soul. It is a believer's search for a deeper, more meaningful practice of faith. "When you pray five times a day, you are automatically connected to God," Zufie said. "This is my 'time out' from the world and this life. I have to believe that this is what keeps me focused on the hereafter and God's bigger plan for us."

She proceeded to outline the challenges of being a British Muslim: the struggle to feel respected at home, at school, and the workplace; also in the most ordinary places, such as the train station, restaurants, and government buildings. We agreed that this dual nature of life, which we had both experienced growing up in Western culture, could contribute to a misunderstanding of a girl's role in mainstream society.

Looking back at my childhood, I learned to live in solitude and accept a level of loneliness and emotions unspoken but written. Before I discovered the love of God, writing became my life-saving ritual. I remember my first short story, "The Seed," written in kindergarten with a simple drawing of the roots of a tree, reflecting my desire to grow freely without cultural apartheid and rituals that had little meaning to a girl in Texas. My entire childhood was spent discovering, defining, and then redefining my own identity. I grew up before there were iPhones or the Internet. The few books about Islam that I found on my father's shelf, such as *The Reconstruction of Religious Thought*, by Dr. Muhammad Iqbal—who happened to be Pakistan's spiritual founder—were too difficult for my young brain to comprehend. So I turned to nature and found God in moon-filled nights when the sky turned silver, lighting up green-black grass, and whispered, *God, You are always here.*

Raised by a strong-willed mother and a traditional father, I had the constant stress of having to please my parents, and that pressure could be overwhelming for a girl like me who learned English at age ten. As a young girl, I remember being allowed to swim in a bathing suit, wear shorts, and play with boys in the neighborhood until I grew up. To be a "good" Muslim girl, I had to respect family and the culture of a country I did not really belong to. Back then, I did not even know that *Islam* is the Arabic word for "peace" and to be a Muslim is to submit to the will of God. At a young age, I had only to submit to a father.

Despite the rules, my parents were fairly liberal-minded. I had bouts of freedom. I could run barefoot in the dirt, go roller-skating, play with my dog Sam for hours, and skip my prayers when I was at school or not pray at all. So long as I had good grades and no boyfriend, I was left alone. If I had secrets to keep, they were recorded in a pile of journals, the uncensored thoughts of a young girl archived in hundreds of pages, tucked away neatly under the bed.

Growing up, I had my own identity struggle—how to be a Muslim, American, or Punjabi confused me on most days. Though I had no real exposure to abuse, war, or violence, except for an occasional news report, I had parents who gifted me with their knowledge and the right to dream of a bright future. Thanks to my father, I was encouraged to pursue activities outside of school and the home. His love and respect for the values and people of the West helped me appreciate the "other" culture, and my only goal in life was to be a professional woman. My young heart believed in the American dream, a goal that my parents worked tirelessly to give to their three children.

And yet, as a young Muslim girl, I endured a deep and personal conflict: trying to belong to two different cultures had left a void that I wanted to ignore by focusing on school. Because I had no structured education in Islam, I could not connect to the sacred verses that Mama sometimes forced me to memorize. How could I commit to memory what I did not understand? Looking back, I recognize that I had no relationship with the Quran. With great difficulty, at the age of fourteen, I learned the verses that a Muslim recites during prayer from a grandmother who once visited from Pakistan. I fasted with my mother and sister each year during the sacred month of Ramadan, despite the scorching Texas sun, to prove that I could live without food and water.

Even though I had yet to learn and read the Quran in its original language, my young heart believed that Heaven was a place beyond the powder-blue skies and pumpkin sun. And this is what all the ISIS girls are hoping for. Their present view of the world as chaotic, confusing, and complex drives them toward a simpler and more tyrannical practice of faith. I could understand the girls' need to belong, to assume an identity greater than oneself, to find purpose and passion to live and, most of all, to be loved.

According to one oral tradition, translated by Kabir Helminski, "You will not enter paradise until you believe, and you will not believe until you love one another." Sadly, the females in radical groups nurture a selective love. In the publication *Till Martyrdom*

*Do Us Part*, published by the Institute of Strategic Dialogue (ISD), authors Erin Marie Saltman and Melanie Smith offer examples of love lost when a male fighter dies shortly after marrying a Western girl.[3] Saltman spent years studying right-wing groups, including religious extremists. Created by Sasha Havlicek, ISD is committed to combating extremism globally.

In ISD's London office, Saltman told me, "The numbers of girls joining ISIS are imperfect. Many girls are not reported or found." Other scholars confirm that the number is in the hundreds rather than the thousands, though we don't have an exact estimate of how many girls join violent groups. An ISD report indicated that by 2015, an estimated 4,000 Westerners had traveled to Syria and Iraq, more than 550 of them women and girls, to join ISIS.

Melanie Smith, a young researcher, uses social media sites to track girls joining ISIS and collate this information in a database. A linguist with a graduate degree from King's College in London, she has found that the majority of female recruits originate from the UK, Belgium, and Germany, ranging in age from sixteen to twenty-five. "The younger girls are more active on social media," Smith said, which made sense given the prevalent use of the Internet by teenagers. According to a government source who asked not to be named, of the seven hundred people who joined ISIS, one hundred were women, which Saltman said is a large number that can't be explained by one or two motivations, even when evidence from the girls' tweets, Facebook posts, and blogs seems to suggest that they left their homes for Syria in search of a romantic destiny. However, the girls' online messages also confirmed that they understood that life in war-torn Syria required great sacrifices.

"There are no unidimensional reasons for why women join ISIS. Some have an obsession with being a good wife or mother, but we've noticed that the younger girls are hyper-engaged with the news; they are looking for adventure, rebellion, and belonging to a sacred culture," Smith said.

So much of what Saltman and Smith shared with me that crisp October morning was convincing and confirmed my own research into the trends of radical women over twenty years. Yes, the girls are more than "jihadi brides." Like their men, they are looking for opportunities to help Muslims in need. Going to Syria to join a cause and support, or fight alongside, men is an act of charity. Islam emphasizes charity throughout the Quran, which is one of the most powerful narratives used by extremists to lure girls into their organization.

In *Till Martyrdom Do Us Part*, Saltman and Smith included the story of a sixteen-year-old Somali girl, Zahra Halane, from the Manchester area in the UK, who celebrated the death of her nineteen-year-old husband from Coventry, who was reportedly killed in December 2014. On Twitter, Halane posted, "He was a blessing from Allah please make dua [prayer] Allah accepts him and I will join him very sooooon."

Halane's twin sister, Salma, had the same feeling about her own husband's death. She tweeted, "May Allah accept my husband, Abu Handhia Al Khrassani rahimullah! I am among the wives of shu-hadah [martyrdom] and I'm honoured to be chosen." The sisters called themselves "wives of the green bird," a common reference to Paradise. In Islam, green is the color of equilibrium, a symbol of fertility, youth, and joy. In the Quran, the blessed will wear green in the Garden of Eden, a green death is the gentlest of all deaths, and the souls of martyrs will fly to Heaven in the form of green birds.

In my own research, I have met women who boasted of martyrdom for themselves and their husbands. "If your husband dies, that makes you a widow," I said to the women I interviewed.

"No. His death makes me the most honorable woman in Islam," they responded, without regret or remorse. For the girls of ISIS, marriage is short-lived, and love is secondary to fulfilling the Caliph's dream of creating a state where women serve their men and procreate. And when a husband dies, there is no time to mourn. Marriage to a new fighter happens quickly, and the cycle of bondage continues.

❋

In the background, classical Turkish music drowned out the noise of other families seated at a near distance. The sound of the lute reminded me of the Ottoman relics I had seen on trips to Turkey—I had been invited on three occasions to give talks on terrorism. One of the lectures was to the Turkish Police Academy in the idyllic seaside town of Antalya. Today, Turkey is a country I avoid traveling to, given the number of terrorist attacks conducted by ISIS in public places, including the airport. In just one decade, the once-peaceful Mediterranean country that straddled both the East and the West became a terrorist target.

After dinner, Zufie and I walked quickly through the cold blue-black night. It was the dead of winter. We stopped along the way for hot chocolate and continued until we arrived at her family's gate. We crossed the courtyard and went inside the three-story historic home that Zufie shared with her aging parents and single brother.

Still talking, we settled on a sofa in the living room. Zufie described her travels to Jordan and Syria before the vicious civil war erupted between the Assad regime, ISIS, and Western-backed rebels. With a master's degree in Arabic from a university in Jordan, Zufie spent three summers, from 2007 to 2009, in Damascus, Syria, practicing the language and wandering through the ancient city. "The city was amazing; with so much history, I could see Islam everywhere. The people were wonderful, so hospitable and so caring.

"Damascus has never been a modern place," she said. Zufie fell in love with the city's gray, utilitarian architecture and cobblestoned streets. She looked past the anticolonial and socialist brand of Syria, ruled by the Ba'ath Party for more than three decades. In her travels, she found Shaykh Nuh, the saint-scholar who guided her deeper into faith.

"The Shaykh says listen with your heart. I had the gift of learning from a disciplined soul," Zufie told me.

Most Muslims believe in the opening of the heart to receive God's divine guidance. The peace-loving Sufis, known as modern-day mystics, use the heart metaphor to elaborate on each of the five points in the organ to seek spiritual power. When I trained the US military, I described the differences between Sunni, Shia, and Sufi Islam. Of the three, Sufis are not a sect. They are a *practice*; their connectedness to God is without ritual, but in meditation, breathing exercises, and poetic verse. For some Sufis, the community is essential. For others, isolation is the divine journey.

Zufie jumped to the call of her mother's voice, resounding from upstairs. She returned with more hot cocoa and halal marshmallows. As always, there was no end to our conversation, only the recognition that the madness of girls joining ISIS could not be entirely explained by ignorant faith alone. That faith, a powerful reason for some to alter their present lives for something more impermanent and unpredictable, had to be combined with other risk factors, or what psychologists call "sensitive periods," when a child is particularly susceptible to environmental factors that are outside the control of her parents. After all, who knew that the girls were spending hours online, day after day, until they crawled into the ISIS narrative? Theirs was not a leap of faith, as it was a culmination of negative experiences, events, and/or emotions that could slowly compel *anyone* into the extremists' trap. In psychopathology, the slow trend toward a specific outcome can be triggered by "turning points" or development experiences, such as joining the military, having a child, or meeting a spouse. All of these add meaning to life.

Conversely, a sequence of unfavorable or hostile experiences in a child's life, which psychopathology points to as causes of abnormal behavior, explains why some children choose violent groups. This is what extremists do best: alter a child's mind through the use of simple declarative religion-laden messages delivered like individual frames in a film. It is the reshaping of a nonviolent child with constant exposure to images of innocent Muslims dying in flames like birds on fire and the pounding conviction that life here on Earth is short, but the Afterlife is an eternal sanctuary for believers.

All Muslims believe in the concept of Paradise. The Quran, oral traditions (hadith literature, the sayings of Prophet Muhammad), and a plethora of scholarly writings outline the joys of Heaven for those who strive, struggle, and sacrifice in *this* life in exchange for *that* life—the only place where a believer can find a perfect, simple, ferocious love without family drama or complexity; the human desire for an endless supply of hope; a place unburdened by heart-numbing sadness or the swelling of secrets in war; and an abundance of empathy. The Other-life is more precious, prized, and loved, reserved for those, as many Muslims believe, who are God-fearing, pious devotees.

The night began to shift into early dawn. The cozy glow of candles in the darkness faded, and the strings of holiday lights outside disappeared as the morning sun illuminated the living room. "It's time," Zufie said in a voice as light as a whisper.

The call to morning prayer sounded from a cell phone programmed to the *adhan*, a male voice reciting a repetition of Arabic words to awaken those sleeping through the night to rise, to pray, to remember and honor God, the Creator of all things. The hazy gray-blue sky slowly faded as a bright miniature sun forced its way onto the chilled horizon. The mineral cold of an English winter had stripped trees of their robe of leaves, the space between them unveiled as the sun painted the sky a dozen shades of pink.

We washed our faces, arms, hands, and feet in lukewarm water in a cleansing ritual known as the *wudu*. We prayed together. I could hear Zufie reciting the memorized verses in a sharp whisper and the sound of feet moving up and down the steps. Everyone was awake.

By late morning, I was on the train heading to Oxford Street. I jotted down the emotional response that Zufie gave to my question about the purpose of our lives: "God has a plan. We are born to be good and to do good. We have to believe that the good in us will survive."

I agreed. The self-centered agenda of extremists was devoid of love. Their narrative logic that violence leads to a political solution and a spiritual renewal is a misreading of Islam. Peaceful and practicing Muslims needed to speak from the truest parts of themselves to help children resist terrorist recruiters. The unimaginable essence of who we are persists beyond these people who are blinded by the fallacy that peace can be achieved through violence.

Beneath their mask of absolute confidence lies an open wound: extremists are incapable of knowing romantic love or love for the sake of God, *fi sabil Allah*, a powerful phrase that connects the believer to the Creator through honest worship, hopeful living, and a healthy dose of compassion for everyone.

Chapter Eight

# WIRED

## *The Internet*

At speaking events, I'm often asked how one connects with religious extremists online. It's simple, I tell them. Search for propaganda films on YouTube. Click on the film and hit the "Like" button. Or find comments posted on Twitter, Facebook, and other social media sites that call individuals to brave death for a cause by migrating to Syria to fight for injustice toward Muslims. In the virtual world, girls are alone, open to strangers, and free to be a different person. With enough clicks and posts, as well as questions about conflicts in the Muslim world, it is relatively easy for a male or female terrorist recruiter to flag a potential recruit. Often, girls take pseudonyms that begin with *Umm* for "mother" in Arabic, even when they are not yet married and have no children. It is a symbol of what's to come, of the new life they will pursue in the land of martyrdom.

Girls create fictional accounts to hide their true identities and intentions. It's also the easiest way for them to conceal their online activities from their parents. With "transient anonymity," a term coined by Jaron Lanier in *You Are Not a Gadget*, girls are uninhibited on the Internet. In their hyperconnectivity, they are free, spending hours of time away from the real world. This organic communication gives Muslim teenage girls looking for a purpose that includes marriage and martyrdom an online community of extremists, who are always available, accessible, and approachable. Since 2016, at least one hundred girls from Western countries have attempted to migrate to Syria.

The London girls were certainly not the first to join ISIS from Europe; security experts report that they were among at least fifty other young women to radicalize in 2015. The news of the missing Muslim girls sent shockwaves throughout the Muslim community in London, as well as the world, raising the question: Why and how did this happen? I remember the image of the three girls on the video camera footage the day of their departure from London's Gatwick Airport, dressed in fashionable winter clothing, and then again in a short video clip of the three girls released in March 2015, only a month later, as they were gathering their luggage and stylish handbags in the southeastern Turkish city of Gaziantep, just north of Aleppo, Syria. That video confirmed to the world that the girls had made their way into ISIS territory. Their disguise and deceit had worked. The girls proved to other girls contemplating the long journey from Western countries that anything was possible, if planned correctly—a journey that began by clicking a button on the Internet.

The three girls in the UK had known each other for years. They had attended the Bethnal Green Academy in southeast London, a haven for immigrants. In the 1880s, Huguenots and Jews from France migrated to this area. These refugees included Ashkenazi from Eastern European countries such as Poland. In East London, easily accessible by the Thames and Lea Rivers, commerce depended on shipbuilding, which also attracted the first wave of migrants from Bangladesh during the British colonial rule of the Indian subcontinent. The would-be ISIS brides lived in the district of Tower Hamlets, mostly inhabited by residents of South Asian origin. The Bethnal Green Academy has a diverse ethnic student population. Three-quarters of the students speak another language other than English.

Of the three teenage girls, fifteen-year-old Shamima Begum was the youngest. A very pretty girl, she was known to be quiet, timid, and seemingly close to her family. She slept in the same bed as her mother, stayed home, and went online when she came home from school. Analysis of Begum's tweets and hashtags showed that the teenager was following at least seventy extremists. Her home life showed signs of trouble and trauma. When her mother died of lung cancer, she moved into her grandmother's house and then moved in with her father, following his remarriage less than two years after the family's tragedy.

The trail of radicalization extends backward from Begum to Aqsa Mahmood, the recruiter whom Begum contacted, a woman who left for Syria when she was nineteen years old. Mahmood, who had been privately educated in Glasgow, persuaded British Muslim girls to migrate to Syria. On Twitter, Mahmood asked Begum to send her a DM, or direct message, before she left her home. Using the moniker Umm Layth ("Mother of the Lion"), Mahmood became *the* most important millennial *muhajirah*, or migrant, and propagandist for ISIS. "Our role is even more important as women in Islam, since if we don't have sisters with the correct *aqeedah* [morals] and understanding who are willing to sacrifice all their desires and give up their families and lives in the West in order to make *hijrah* [the journey to Syria] and please Allah, then who will raise the next generation of lions?" she posted online.

Mahmood, a beautiful South Asian girl, had been in touch with a male ISIS recruiter who groomed the Scottish resident for months. Her mother, Khalida Mahmood, told the press that she found a suspicious text from an English-based ISIS recruiter, Adeel ul-Haq, on her daughter's mobile phone in May 2013, just six months before Mahmood's escape to Syria via Turkey. Only after ul-Haq was jailed and began serving a six-year sentence for recruiting girls like Mahmood did the family tell the press that they had spotted signs of radicalization, but it's unclear how or if the parents tried to stop her. Her father said, "They [ISIS men] prey on the vulnerable, brainwash the kids, then break them from their families and, of course, it's all a secret and exciting for the young people until it's too late."

In a CNN interview, the father said that Mahmood "was the best daughter we could have, and we don't know what happened to her, no." According to her parents, Mahmood was a model child from a loving family. She was studying medicine. She liked Western things: Coldplay, cosmetics, and *Harry Potter*. Unlike the UK girls who went to Syria, who were raised in an immigrant neighborhood in East London, Mahmood grew up in Pollokshields, a placid residential suburb in southwest Glasglow. Mahmood's father went to Scotland in the 1970s; a former famous cricket player from Pakistan before he settled in the West, he opened a successful line of hotels, earning enough to raise a family of four children. He paid for his daughter's tuition at private school. Known for her ambition and attention, Mahmood went to Shawlands Academy and then enrolled at Glasgow Caledonian University to study diagnostic radiotherapy.

There are few details about her social life except from her online messages. In social media, she talked about the pressures of her family to do well and the evils of feminism that force young women to want material things. Once a fan of J.K. Rowling's fictional boy wizard character, Mahmood denounced Rowling's creation as pagan. She dropped out of university in her second year and expressed anger at the Syrian regime's treatment of Muslims. On Twitter, her circle of friends expanded; she followed blogs and sites that reinforced a destructive worldview.

Two days before Mahmood left home, she persuaded two friends to go to Glasgow's Buchanan Street bus station and store a rucksack for her in a locker. Not knowing what was in it or why, they agreed. Inside was everything Mahmood needed for her one-way journey to Syria: a plane ticket, money, toiletries, and clothes.

Then she disappeared.

Three months later, Mahmood called her parents from Syria and told them her plan had worked: their prospective son-in-law was an ISIS fighter. She promised her family that she would meet them in Heaven.

I can't imagine the pain of her mother, who, after learning of her daughter's escape, said, "I never slept, I felt as though I was dying. My children, my in-laws, my husband, every one of us, cried through the night. My baby had gone and nobody was doing anything to stop it."

I certainly don't know what the parents should or could have done to prevent their daughter from sliding down the slippery slope of savagery. Could the mother have taken away the phone? Or stopped her daughter from chatting with a strange man? Did the parents allow Mahmood to have friends outside the home and her extended family? Did the girl feel restrained, restricted, or reserved? What kind of life did Mahmood have *before* an ISIS recruiter brainwashed her? And why didn't the family see signs of radicalization? Did they notice the change in their daughter's behavior? These are the kinds of questions that are useful, not only to law enforcement agencies, but also to families struggling to keep their children safe from terrorist recruiters.

After Mahmood left Scotland, she helped the British girls prepare for Syria. She sent them a checklist and a step-by-step guide on what they should pack. In electronic messages, Mahmood wrote, "If you are married or plan to marry, you might want to bring things you would like to wear in private. You'll also want to bring clothes for both summer and winter that you can maybe wear around your husband, maybe things that aren't so appropriate around sisters, for example short dresses."

In a post on her Tumblr site, Mahmood told the UK girls to bring beauty products, medication, and electronics, as well as prenatal vitamins and painkillers should they become pregnant. Her list was very specific, including everything from waterproof warm boots in winter to mosquito after-bite cream and spray. She wrote, "If I could advise you to bring one thing it would be organic coconut oil (maybe grab an extra jar for me as well lol). This is such a helpful product with multiuse—body moisturizer/hair oil, etc. . . . and large zip lock bags very useful for keeping things in place as well as travel cases, as you can be living out of your suitcases for months so it helps keep things organized . . . and a charger—they only sell fake phones here [in Syria]." (Mahmood was right about coconut oil—it's the one beauty product I live by.) As one of the few girls who left early for Syria, Mahmood served as a travel and survivor guru to other girls.

A prolific writer online, Mahmood reportedly became a leading figure in the Al-Khansaa Brigade, the feared all-female force in charge of enforcing strict laws on women and children. Among these laws: no woman is allowed outside the home unless accompanied by a male guardian; women must be covered in a full-length veil at all times in a public space; women must not talk to or shake hands with men; women must observe the ban on cosmetics; no woman is allowed to listen to music; women are encouraged to remarry, if a husband dies fighting; and so on. As a leading figure, Mahmood helped other girls coming to Syria adjust to their new lives.

She offered security tips to prevent the London girls from being detected by the police and airport authorities. "Avoid searching things from your home Wifi and devices you plan to bring, this way you have nothing that can be held against you in case you're caught. Don't download anything that could cause suspicion—do all that once you arrive. In fact, I would advise you have things on your devices that could throw the authorities off if they look through them." She reminded the girls to be discreet, telling no one about their journey to Syria, especially the girls' parents. "I can say from experience it's not an easy thing but you need to think of what's best for the people you love," wrote Mahmood, who only called her family after she arrived at the Turkish border in November 2013, four days after her departure. The day she left home, she gave her father a long hug goodbye, saying, *"Khuda hafiz,"* a greeting in Urdu for "May God be with you."

One of the first British Muslim women to travel to Syria was twenty-four-year-old Grace "Khadijah" Dare, who left in 2012 to join ISIS with her baby son, Isa (Arabic for "Jesus"). Born to Nigerian parents, Dare is unrecognizable in photographs when cloaked in black next to her young husband, Abu Bakr, a Swedish man. Unlike the other London girls, Dare was raised as a Christian and converted to Islam in her teens. Dare changed her name to Maryam, the mother of Jesus Christ, and became a prolific social media user, writing under the name "Muhajirah fi Sham" or "immigrant in Syria." She tweeted about ISIS public executions and celebrated the beheading of James Foley. In a propaganda video, Dare is with a young boy named Isa. The little boy is wearing an ISIS headband and says, "We will kill the infidels over there."

Dare set an example for other girls that life—a husband, children, and a home—is possible in war-torn Syria. Online, other women declare their love and desire for marriage and martyrdom.

Writing as Umm Ubaydah, one woman posts, "I wonder if I can pull a Mulan and enter the battlefield," making a reference to the Disney character who defied all odds when she dressed as a man to fight alongside men. A publication by the Institute for Strategic Dialogue titled *Becoming Mulan? Female Western Migrants to ISIS* describes the flow of Western female fighters to Syria and details their day-to-day experiences in the new country.[1] In another post, Umm Ubaydah writes, "We are trying to build an Islamic state that lives and abides by the law of Allah." Other women write about the Afterlife. Umm Khattab says she has "no desire to live in this world [as] her aspiration is the hereafter [because] we love death."

Despite their new lives, some women miss their families. Although Mahmood never returned to Scotland, she admitted that the greatest struggle "in the land of jihad is your family." She wrote a verse for her mother titled "Ya Umee" ("O Mother") on her blog site to express her sorrow for not saying goodbye to her:

> I swear to God preparing yourself to leave [your family] is difficult because you are leaving the woman who kept you in her womb for 9 months . . . even if you know how right this path and decision is and how your love for Allah comes before anything and everything, this is still an ache which only one who has been through and experienced it can understand.

No matter how committed Mahmood was to ISIS, she was conflicted. She knew her family was begging her to return to them. She heard her mother crying on the phone when she called Scotland. She wrote, "I swear to God, it's so hard to hear this and I can never do justice to how cold hearted you feel."

This duality of emotions creates conflicts for some young women, who then try to leave when most cannot. For those who want to escape, it is a heart-wrenching struggle to live one way, with an unshakable belief that Syria is the new land of Islam, and also to know that they had another life, perceived as less spiritual or worthy but one that included their parents, siblings, school, and friends.

Unlike the three UK girls, Mahmood traveled alone. The London girls had each other, and because they were classmates, one former radical told me it was unlikely that they would have gone to Syria on their own. Together, they planned the trip, making a shopping list of items to take with them, and ultimately making the journey together.

Neurologist David Eagleman, in his acclaimed book *The Brain: The Story of You*, offers a physiological reason for why peer pressure strongly compels behavior in teens. He writes,

> Areas involved in social considerations (such as the mPFC) are more strongly coupled to other brain regions that translate motivations into actions (the striatum and its network of connections). This . . . might explain why teens are more likely to take risks when their friends are around. How we see the world as a teenager is the consequence of a changing brain that's right on schedule. These changes lead us to be more self-conscious, more risk-taking, and more prone to peer-motivated behavior. . . . [Therefore,] who we are as a teenager is not simply the result of a choice or an attitude; it is the product of a period of intense and inevitable neural change.[2]

Mahmood used her Tumblr blog, titled "Diary of a Muhajirah" (Arabic for "migrant"), to promulgate her views: "The media at first used to claim that the ones running away to join the Jihad as being unsuccessful, didn't have a future and from broke down families etc. But that is far from the truth. Most sisters I have come across have been in university studying courses with many promising paths, with big, happy families and friend and everything. If we had stayed behind, we could have been blessed with it all from a relaxing and comfortable life and lots of money." Mahmood did not fit the overrated profile once used to identify potential recruits: a low-income or middle-class individual from a broken home who showed signs or symptoms of distress or trauma. She was an example that someone from an entirely opposite background could be susceptible to radical messages.

On Al Jazeera English's *Everywoman* show, I was asked about girls who joined terrorist groups years before ISIS existed. My answer and research at the time focused on women choosing violence as a means of protest. "Women protest the loss of their (male) family members, the loss of their communities and the meltdown of society, and the loss of their homeland," I said. Today, the same argument can be applied to the way girls and women join terrorist groups to protest their mundane, meaningless lives and find meaning in religious extremism. Some protest the current conditions of war and conflict, believing that participation in violence will change the status quo; this could explain why some girls, like Mahmood, express their desire to fight for Muslims in Syria: they want to bring peace and stability to Muslims in a war-torn country. They believe that they are agents of change.

Other girls and women protest the West in general, believing that a puritanical, live-by-the-book way of life is the "true" practice of Islam. Years ago, before the Internet played a major role in radicalizing girls, male recruiters used offline networks and sometimes depended on older women to recruit young women. I remember an earlier website, which has since been deactivated, called *Mujahidaat* ("Female Fighters"), with writings by and for women on how to join violent groups. This was before the takeover by ISIS as the premier extremist group that needed female members to help men create the mythical Muslim state.

At a conference held at Tufts University in Massachusetts several years ago, I gave a presentation on the writings of men to implore women to join religious extremism. Some of these men are now dead, but their written work lives on. Violent extremists and propagandists have released a stream of books, articles, and online publications that target Muslims for siding with the West. On the Internet, the forever vehicle of information, the writings of men are made tangible and are continuously relevant. Al-Qaeda's former leader of operations in the Arabian Peninsula, Shaykh Al-Hafith Yusuf bin Salih al-Uyayri, also known by his nom de guerre Swift Sword, wrote the seminal book on the subject, titled *The Role of the Women in Fighting the Enemies.*[3] He wrote, "The reason we address women . . . is our observation that when a woman is convinced of something, no one will spur a man to fulfill it like she will . . . the saying behind every great man stands a woman was true for Muslim women at these times, for behind every great *mujahid* stood a woman."

In his book, Al-Uyayri cites examples of women from previous battles to convince modern-day women of their instrumental role. He urges women to be "the cradle of the men . . . [and] carry out [their] active role in the current war between Islam and all the disbelieving nations, without exception." He says that without women, men will lose wars.

His counterpart, a cleric in Saudi Arabia named Shaykh ibn Jibreen, issued a *fatwa*, or legal edict, allowing a Muslim woman to participate in jihad on certain conditions: "When if she is fighting the *kuffar* [disbeliever], on foreign territory, and if the act [of violence] will ease her pain and inflict damage on the enemy." At various speaking events, I have been asked if the late kingpin of terrorism, Osama bin Laden, endorsed women in terrorism. While he never called upon women to strap on the bomb, for example, or take up arms, he did recognize the role of women in warfare. In his famous "Declaration of War Against Americans," Bin Laden said, "Our women had set a tremendous example for generosity in the cause of Allah; they motivate and encourage their sons, brothers, and husbands to fight for the cause of Allah in Afghanistan, Bosnia, Chechnya, and in other countries . . . our women encourage jihad."

I have argued this point for years: that women are valuable to male-dominated terror groups for the different roles they play as mother, daughter, and sister to men. Women have allowed male groups to survive; and women, half of any society, are the future of a state built on extreme religious practice. The Islamic State group, al-Qaeda's stepchild, is more aggressively recruiting women than any other terror group and convinces its followers of a utopia that does not exist in Syria—this false narrative is a key political motivator for both men and women.

In the early days of Islam, Muslim women helped their men to victory. They tended to wounded soldiers. They carried messages and money. They called on men to fight to protect Muhammad. They were the mothers of the believers.[4] Women were skilled in warfare. They were given swords to use in fighting by the early Muslim men. One of the most celebrated female fighters was Nusaybah bint Ka'ab, also known as Umm Umarah ("mother of

Umarah"). She fought in Islam's second Battle of Uhud in 625 CE, lost one arm, and suffered eleven wounds as she protected her Prophet.[5] After Muhammad's death, Muslim women continued to fight. A Bedouin woman, Khawlah bint al-Azwar, dressed like a knight and entered the battlefield with other women. She "slashed the head of the Greek," a reference to the Byzantines who retreated after the Muslims declared victory.[6]

What the early women did not do, however, was commit acts of senseless violence. Only those who sacrificed their lives in defense of their honor, their homes, or the Prophet could be called martyrs. In Islamic law, the UK girls and the Scottish propagandist were disqualified as martyrs for joining the Islamic State, a violent group acting only in the name of Islam. The killing of innocent civilians, destruction of property, abuse of non-Muslim women, and suicide operations are all forbidden in Islam.

The eldest of the three London girls, Kadiza Sultana, was sixteen years old. An iconic photograph of Sultana with her two girlfriends is the typical image of ISIS women. But in truth, the girls and women of ISIS are no longer independent. They have been stripped of emotional, physical, and spiritual freedom and live within the confines of Raqqa; their lives, now tragic, will lead to senseless death, which is why some girls and women hope to escape. Sultana was one of those girls who died trying.

Her family lawyer, Tasnime Akunjee, said that Sultana tried to run away from ISIS, which is "like trying to escape Alcatraz." We know that ISIS has brutally killed girls and women planning to escape. Once you're in, there is no going back. The lawyer told a British newspaper, the *Guardian*, that Sultana was probably killed in summer 2015 when an airstrike hit a residential building, most likely from a Russian bomber.[7]

In response to the news of her death, the lawyer told the press, "The family are devastated. A number of sources have said that she has been killed and she has not been in contact with the family for several weeks. Over a year ago, she had been talking about leaving. There was a plan to get her out." Sultana's conversations with her sister suggested that she wanted to leave ISIS. "I don't have a good feeling. I feel scared," she said. "You know the borders are closed right now, so how am I going to get out? Where is Mum? I want to speak to her."

As a mother, I wonder if children who radicalize show signs or tendencies in advance, before taking the leap. In my own lectures, supported by two decades of research, I talk about how this happens. Online recruitment begins in the most benign way. A girl (or boy) expresses interest in Islam, and within hours, if not days, she gains new followers. She becomes part of an ongoing conversation about Islam and events in the Muslim world, including the crisis in Syria. Her interest in conflicts leads her into the ISIS pit—a recruiter eventually finds her. Suddenly, she has new friends—more friends than she could have imagined in the real, offline world. She is part of a larger community, a network of violent followers who have the same desire to belong to a violent extremist group.

A series of events and emotions explain radical behavior. Girls may be overwhelmed with rules and rituals at home. They may feel or actually be socially isolated. They might feel estranged from their families and friends, be marginalized by the school community, be victims of abuse or trauma experienced as a child or a young adult, long for something and someone, have a desire to know their religion, or have been bullied in childhood. Sometimes, girls are shamed if they are found with a boyfriend or take part in illicit sexual affairs. This crippling, burning shame is so toxic that a girl feels she has no option but to join extremism to restore her honor. Growing up Muslim in America, I could understand the difficult experience of having to embrace a mainstream Western culture while obeying the rules of tradition and norms practiced and expected of girls at home. This seeming contradiction between the two different cultures and identities often causes confusion and conflict, and it compels some girls to make unwise choices.

"Being in love, or in a state of infatuation, runs a neurobiology that can rival being on drugs," Dr. Anne Speckhard, an adjunct associate professor of psychiatry in the School of Medicine at Georgetown University and director of the International Center for the Study of Violent Extremism, told me. Love online feels real and is rewarding. *An artificial love affair.* Their desire for romantic fatalism escapes logic. Finally, the girls of ISIS can belong to someone other than their parents. Kalsoom Bashir, codirector of Inspire, an organization dedicated to educating and empowering British Muslim women, is widely interviewed in the UK on the ways young women turn to violence and highlights early signs of radicalization. According to a 2015 *Independent* article, "Speaking on the *Andrew Marr Show*, [Bashir] said the group's 'very specific campaign' was targeting vulnerable young Muslim women and capitalizing on their sense of injustice, isolation, alienation and the struggle between cultural expectations and the demands of a liberal society."[8] This was an all-too-common theme that I heard from young women and girls in my own interviews—their lack of knowledge about Islam coupled with familial and societal pressures can create personal conflict and confusion (e.g., how to be a "good" Muslim).

For years, I have been speaking and writing about the importance of context and culture and why it's important to understand the personal background of each woman or girl who joins violent extremism. Although each case is different—no two Muslim women are alike—there are common themes that explain why some females join ISIS. It could be "religious illiteracy," a term Bashir uses to provoke discussion about Islam in Muslim families and communities to contradict violent propaganda and misinformation about a peaceful religion.[9] Of the barriers that contribute to female radicalization, Bashir believes the lack of religious knowledge in some families and their unwillingness to discuss extremism and religion widens the intergenerational divide. Ignorance of Islam along with cultural expectations for girls to be honorable and homebound can also contribute to the difficulties they face when expected to live in two very different worlds—one that is faith-based while the other is secular and Western.[10] Other barriers for females include the lack of "strong credible Muslim leadership" and fear of challenging the extremists' hateful narratives.[11]

Since 2000, Bashir has committed herself to educating the youth. As a former Muslim chaplain at the University of Bristol, she helped improve the rights of students: equality, freedom of speech, the right to study, the right to question, the right to be protected from prejudice and extremism, and the right to live in a safe and nurturing environment. In her work, Bashir believes in strengthening the Muslim youth through education from credible Muslim sources. In an article for *Inspire*, she writes, "Education is the cornerstone of our society. It is crucial to building the knowledge and skills of our young people, and also in nurturing their values and beliefs."[12] That education should include learning and understanding Islam as a peaceful, loving religion, which involves critical thinking skills.

Bashir continues, "Teaching students to constantly question what they are told or shown is so important in developing the skills needed to resist those who aim to force ideas and values upon them. . . . My concern is that in our misguided anxiety not to offend, we actually risk failing those who we should be helping to protect. Extremist ideologies, unless challenged, can find fertile breeding grounds among vulnerable members of society."[13]

Learning about Islam online or from unlearned Muslims is a dangerous trend. Rather than turn to a born-again-shaykh on the Internet, it's absolutely essential to seek information from credible sources, scholars and educated Muslims who have a nonliteral approach to faith. Luckily, being raised in America and gifted with a secular education, I had the right to question everything about faith: What is the meaning of jihad? Why do Muslims pray? What is the purpose of fasting? What is the path to Heaven? And much more. However, for many Muslim girls and boys in ultraconservative families, questioning the faith is perceived as blasphemous, bad-mannered, and, at its extreme, sacrilegious.

Therefore, questioning authority is not always accepted. I know this from presenting my own questions to imams and scholars throughout the Muslim world. Ultraconservatives argue that questions about scripture, law, and oral traditions cannot be asked. Bashir has spent her adult life trying to answer some of the most difficult questions, or at least find answers to them. In order to empower the youth and women, she wants women to know that they are equal to men in the eyes of God. Like Bashir, I believe that educating women and girls on their rights in Islam can empower them against violent extremists, Islamophobes, and ultraconservative men and women.

Working with Bashir is her partner and the codirector of Inspire, Sara Khan, who is an award-winning counter-extremism and women's rights campaigner. In January 2018, Khan was appointed lead commissioner for the newly created Commission for Countering Extremism by British Home Secretary Amber Rudd. Khan is unafraid of the hard-line Muslims who defame her for her opinions. Interviewed by the *Sunday Times* in an article titled "I'm taking on the Islamists. But where's your backbone?"[14] Khan is not concerned by the threats she receives and the abusive messages on social media—threats of gang rape or death. Her new book, *The Battle for British Islam: Reclaiming Muslim Identity from Extremism*, is peppered with stories such as one about a thirteen-year-old girl from Birmingham—an hour's drive from London, with a diverse and divided Muslim population—who was radicalized online and believed that Syria should be an "Islamic Disneyland."[15] Khan says the girl's behavior was flagged early enough, and she is now back in school. Her story reminded me of the East African girls in Denver, which I discussed in chapter 5. The girls were captured on their way to Syria and returned to their families. They, too, went back to school again.

In the UK, the government and law enforcement agencies are actively involved with local Muslim communities to prevent radicalization. A leading activist in Birmingham and radio talk show host named Ahmad Bostan believes in the UK government's goodwill to address the risks of radicalization in the Muslim community, despite the backlash. In his kind voice, Bostan told me, "First of all, terrorism and extremism are dealt with in different ways. The government has allocated separate funding and separate initiatives to deal with extremism under the Stronger Britain Together campaign and the Prevent strategy." We agreed that the principles of the government's programs, such as tackling terrorism and protecting society, are also based on Islamic values.

Birmingham is the UK's second-largest city. Famous for its musical scene, the densely populated city boasts of ethnic diversity. Emerging from an average eighteenth-century market town as the birthplace of the "Midlands Enlightenment," the city became one of the country's first manufacturing towns and today is the fourth most visited city in England by international visitors. A native of Birmingham, Bostan described for me the different Muslim communities, some of which he believes to be intolerant of other Muslims and the British way of life:

> A huge tragedy we've had in this country [the UK] is how our mosques and madrasas are regulated. The reality is that they're not regulated and that has been a problem for a very long time. We have girls and women who go to the mosque and madrasa and are taught Islam, perhaps for a few hours every day, and there is no way to know what they are learning, and what interpretation of Islam is preached. What do we know about the teachers? Do the teachers have a previous criminal record? Many of the Muslim teachers come from overseas countries, and it's important to know their background, the practice of Islam, and their views of women.[16]

Bostan believes that male community leaders have a responsibility to provide opportunities for women.

> The title of the community leader is used too often, when the central problem is that we don't have enough women coming forth and taking leadership positions in the Muslim community. We, as a community, are not doing enough to put women forward, which is a major issue. . . . It results in young women growing up with a serious lack of role models from their religious community.

Bostan began his first radio show when he was eleven years old. Now in his twenties, he's an experienced television host. Bostan encourages dialogue on the most sensitive issues: women's rights, ultraconservative preachers, and the rise of religious extremism. An irrational interpretation of Islam with a moderate mask feeds the hard-line narrative that bars Muslim girls from achieving success.

> Girls grow up with this idea that they are inferior to men, that Islam dictates this, that they have certain shortcomings or

insufficiencies that come from their faith. As a result, girls are searching for answers. When they go to the mosque, they are taught the Quran and the hadith but they don't know what the Quran means. They don't know the context of the oral traditions. So, when ISIS comes along and offers a translation of the Quran that empowers girls, then they no longer feel inferior or insufficient. They don't think they are a lesser class than men.

Bostan blames the narrow, literalist, and Wahhabi doctrine for the radicalization of girls and young women in Europe. "Historically when we speak about Wahhabism, it is in the context of the Middle East and North Africa, but now we see an increasing number of women and girls from South Asian communities being drawn to this ideology, and that is new."

The challenge lies with identifying the *right* people, Bostan continued. "It's important for Muslims to be passionate about fighting extremism and to come forward and work with women. We have a lot of self-appointed leaders in the community, but we need people who live normal lives as Muslims in the UK. They are proud to be British, confident in faith, and stand up for girls and women's rights."

*What does engagement look like online?* I wondered. It seemed clear to me that extremists' narratives were easily recognizable—we know hate when we see (or feel) it. Countering hateful ideologies falls under an entire field of study called "strategic communications" that develops the stories, messages, and images that reinforce true Islam and rejects ISIS's use of narratives to seduce its followers. For years, I have been working with various local and international partners to implement programs and strategies to defeat the violent narratives that come from religious extremists.

On my desk is a propaganda guide from March 1990 written in Peshawar, a northern town in Pakistan. Titled *On the Jihadi Media: How to Communicate with the Public*, it is infused with misquoted scripture and a list of communication tools to reach the Muslim population. These tools include pamphlets, posters, printed slogans, cassette tapes, radio, rumors, and more. Some of the earlier tools are outdated, but the need to influence populations is the same. Long ago, extremists recognized the power of media messages and the importance of their distribution and delivery. Today, we know that extremists are tech-savvy, broadcasting their messages via online newsletters, communiqués, blogs, and a wide range of social media sites. Their reach is unlimited and their mastery of the Internet inexhaustible. In 2015, ISIS released a newsletter titled *How to Survive in the West*, encouraging the use of propaganda to gain public support and providing lessons in Internet privacy: "Your normal Internet activity might consist of you checking your emails, playing some games, searching for recipes etc. All this will ensure you are 'clean.' Nothing guilty can be traced to your IP address."

Laura Scaife, a lawyer and technology consultant, offers a practical approach to engaging young people before they radicalize.

> There is so much content generated every day [online]. There needs to be more done to filter it . . . and we need more involvement from the government. Let's say you search for anything on terrorism or terrorism-related material online, it's important to see something that will encourage you to think again, with different arguments to challenge the views you might have. A lot of this is tied to Google Advertising, where they can encourage people from the first page rather than page seven of extremist content. We need to make sure we have access to the counter-narrative or at least balance what girls are informed of and what they search for.[17]

Others have argued that this approach is an infringement on an individual's right to privacy and an attack on freedom of speech. But Scaife believes that social media intervention is necessary to protect young people from being exposed to extremist messages. She said, "Social media sites need to be more active in developing tools to facilitate the process; there needs to be more discussion on how surveillance works and what the government can do to search results of young people online. . . . There is a very negative public perception and a lack of general understanding on how cybersecurity works."

While online surveillance is controversial, proponents argue that it's the only way for governments to know what curious teenagers are viewing. In her own guide, Scaife made a list of social media sites that young people should avoid. "I can't get anyone in the UK government to engage me on this issue. Not a lot of government departments believe it's in their remit or you get ignored," she said.

A single-path solution is simplistic. Helping young people to be Internet-safe is one way to manage their online fake friendships and activities. In my lectures, I have emphasized the need to strengthen Muslim families, a priority for community leaders, government programs, faith-based groups, and schools. We know that in the absence of strong families, girls turn to other authority figures. Many girls who feel isolated at home by their parents from the broader community turn to the online space for safety, sex, and a sweetheart.

In the short term, parents can give their girls more freedom and the opportunity to maintain an open and loving relationship with them at home that provides an environment without fear of punishment for wrongs committed or thoughts revealed. In my work, I have interviewed numerous girls who are afraid of their parents, too scared to tell them what they need. One girl expressed her desire to be an artist. Her father disagreed, and the mother, submissive to her husband, said nothing. Before the girl turned twenty, she was married to a man twice her age and then later taken from her husband's home by her overbearing brother for reasons that remain unknown. In less than a year, she was divorced from a man she scarcely knew. Years later, this girl, now a thirty-something woman, is half-mad. She screams at the wall, fights with her mother for trying to force her into another marriage, and turns to painting once again, in silence. That woman is my cousin.

In the long term, Islam is countering violent extremism. I speak openly about the need to connect with the Quran; to learn the intricate meaning of scripture; to understand the context of revelations; to live with charity, compassion, and concern for one's immediate community; and to avoid Google Shaykh.

Chapter Nine

# SOUL SICK

*Afghanistan*

Lisa clutched her nine-millimeter weapon as insurgents fired into the house of men, women, and children. A team of US soldiers and Special Forces operators engaged in one of the worst firefights that had taken place in Wardak province; this central east region of Afghanistan was the scene of some of the most violent battles launched by violent extremists. Trapped by intense hostile fire, US forces battled a local Afghan insurgent group named Hezb-e-Islami (HIG), or Party of Islam.

"There were fourteen people in the house, including four children. The women were in the back of the room," Lisa told me in an interview.

The event took place in a small village. On the right side of the room in the back of the house, a local woman concealed by her clothing stood near a large propane tank. As insurgents continued to fire at American soldiers, an explosion hit the house. Lisa was blown out the front door. The suicide bomber killed four children and two American servicemen.

Lisa tried to stay calm as she shared her story. The memory of the female suicide bomber made her voice crack. Her eyes welled with tears. Her simple declarative sentences were like individual frames in a film.

"She was a nobody [to the men], a nomad from Pakistan who was moving weapons for the Taliban and the HIG. She was pushed outside of her tribe when her [Afghan] husband was killed."

Before 2010, local insurgents didn't include or invite women into their groups. Committing acts of violence was reserved for men. But that began to change when men became desperate and decided to recruit women to attack Americans. Insurgents operate from bone-white mountains in a parched, defeated land. Along the switchback mountain roads, the Kuchi, the Dari word for "nomad"—are always moving, with their camels, goats, sheep, and children. The women wear dazzling plum, yellow, and red dresses speckled with sequins and mirrors. To the outsider, the Kuchi are a people without borders or boundaries. Their life romanticized by Western historians, Kuchis are Pashtuns, the dominant tribe in Afghanistan, some now settled in cities and villages.

Nomads are convenient pawns for insurgents. They depend on them to move their weapons. Because the Kuchis are always moving, they are unsuspected collaborators. Sometimes, women act as facilitators and messengers. Few are killers. I knew from studying women in war that they are not involved in fighting. Female bombers are uncommon.

As a woman, Lisa was able to speak to the Kuchi women to glean information on the insurgents' communications. She suspected that the nomads had knowledge of insurgent activity; they could be wives of the insurgents.

"I couldn't get to the bomber quick enough," she said.

For years, I had listened to stories like this: survivors of tragedy, grateful to be alive, never forget that frightening, dark moment. American novelist William Faulkner once wrote, "The past is never dead. It's not even past."[1] Lisa had a collection of memories from her deployments to Afghanistan, but that one harrowing event seemed to be life-changing for her. Because she survived.

"These women do what they are told. What they know is to hate us because they don't know us," Lisa said.

There can be few places as hostile as Afghanistan, between the scorching sun of summer and the piercing subzero winds of winter. In some parts of the country, the landscape is drained of all color except white and patches of beige. Other provinces reveal shades of lime green and placid water. To the outsider, the daily carnage is so singularly unspectacular, so primitive. As if conflict were familiar to the country and the people were accustomed to certain expectations—violent displacements, unfit rulers, and the silence of grief.

In a country defined by stereotypes, eye-catching pictures of Afghan girls and stories of women tormented by conflict have captured our imagination. Consider Steve McCurry's iconic photograph of the girl with green eyes, her unruly brown hair half-covered in a crimson shawl—this single image of an Afghan girl in tattered clothing from the cover of the June 1985 *National Geographic* revealed a nation haunted by war. Or the stories told by American-Afghan physician-turned-novelist Khaled Hosseini, widely known for his huge best seller *The Kite Runner*, who explores the lives of mothers and daughters in *A Thousand Splendid Suns*, a heartbreaking saga of women afflicted by Afghanistan's violent history.

Lisa continued, "I tried to understand why this woman did what she did. We found out that when her husband was killed, she was pushed outside of her tribe. She had two male children. She looked old and harsh. I guessed she was over forty. She had years on her face. In that culture, when a woman loses her husband, she loses everything. Men take advantage of a woman's loss in order to further the insurgency. They use her vulnerability, and it increases her anger and hatred for us.

"This is a scary trend. Men are learning how to use women in a country where it's against the cultural norm for women to step outside the home. I believe the woman was desperate. She had no home. She had no tribe. So, she chose revenge."

Anger is an intense emotion. And because it's a powerful emotion, it demands an equally powerful response. Psychologists describe anger as an attack against someone or something. I have seen anger on the faces of women in conflict, whose inevitable, necessary madness leads them to an unbound darkness. The result is an unhealthy response to overcome the pain of loss.

The complete identity of the female bomber is sometimes unknown. Even when female operatives are named, they are slippery characters. Their lives are fragmented and distorted by half-truths reported in the media or by their families. For the weak, wearing death as a dress is a desirable personal choice. Lisa believed that the woman who nearly killed her was emotionally bruised.

"I couldn't save her."

"It's not easy to save every woman," I said. "You must trust that God is watching over them."

For a moment, she had an expression of rage, a searing emotion: the feeling of helplessness, of being abandoned and not knowing how to rescue the desperate Afghan woman. Perhaps Lisa thought she could do something, just *something*, rather than betray her conscience with the illusion of helping a people she barely knew. Here there were no abstractions; here was flesh and blood, the unmistakable truth of vulnerability that ended the lives of one woman and the soldiers Lisa had known, lives lost to senseless violence in a place where the sky can be pink with purple clouds at sunset, and the water can go from emerald to deep indigo under the light of a half-moon. *Afghanistan is still wild and beautiful.* I wondered how women coped with the spell of conflict in a place thickened with silence, the memories of war confined to the slow-moving front of time.

Lisa refuted the stereotypes of women seduced by the severity and savagery of decades-long fighting. On the other side of war, she discovered women with emotional power: an affection and attachment to one another, their grace and goodness reflected in small acts of charity. The more I listened to Lisa, the more I understood that Afghan women were diverse, different, and determined to survive, despite the odds against them. In her own personal journey through Afghanistan, author Christina Lamb discovered the brave writers of the province of Herat, who risked their lives to carry on a literary tradition under the guise of sewing circles.[2]

During one of my talks on Islam, I met Lisa at Fort Hood, Texas. Outside the auditorium, Lisa introduced herself to me as a senior officer in the US Army leading missions in Afghanistan. I remember her trusting eyes, pained with a brutal truth: she could not save the fallen victims of Afghanistan. In that single moment, I learned enough about the personal tragedies in her life. She later told me that she grew up in the South, raised by her mother, who was widowed and poor. A man she loved ran away or died. She raised three boys with the help of her mother. Two sons went to war and died in battle.

"When my boys were killed, life got simple," she said.

Her youngest son lives with his grandmother. Her second love, a man from Afghanistan, betrayed her, and the short-lived marriage ended badly. She was now on her own.

When I returned to Virginia, Lisa and I met a few times a year, sharing food and chai in each other's homes. Her photographs of Afghanistan portrayed a country of ravaged magnificence: alluvial plains funneled upward to the dove-white mountain peaks; leafless trees bathed in a mango sun; wisps of snow buried the living green under a silver-black night sky; and women with brilliant blue eyes large as leaves were revealed when the all-covering veil was removed. Lisa also told me what I suspected to be true: the continuity of blasts and gunfire created an irrational, possessing anxiety for American soldiers returning home.

So long as the war continued, the exchange of manic, almost uncontrollable fire would invite more extremism, the terrorist attacks, the crisis of leadership, and the conflict with the Taliban. This is how the world knows Afghanistan. In few places is death as widespread. Children born there have the bleakest futures. According to one report, Afghanistan is the fourth most dangerous country in the world.[3] Other surveys list the country as the worst place for women, who are at high risk for health threats, sexual violence, oppression from cultural and religious traditions, lack of access to legal recourse, human trafficking, and systematic rape.

Perhaps the greatest threat of all to Afghan women is their family. Women experience forced marriage and physical, sexual, and psychological abuse at the hands of men. "It's a question of control and power. You use religion, you use culture, you use tradition, you use gender to keep the power, to keep control," said Sima Samar, women's rights activist and chairperson of the Afghanistan Independent Human Rights Commission, in an interview with Al Jazeera.

The female bomber's death was not the end of the story. There would be more women to follow. These stories were painful to hear, but they had become imaginable. My former students who had been deployed once or twice to Afghanistan shared their own experiences with female bombers. The women, hidden behind thick clothing, pretending to be innocent victims of war, target Americans and Afghan nationals in acts of vengeance. These women rarely make television news headlines. Their identities are enshrouded in secrecy, their lives largely unknown to local authorities.

At times, it was difficult to listen to the stories of these women who are burdened by a place that is corrupt, unsettling, a cobweb of crises and self-contained chaos. One afternoon as I listened to Lisa, I had a mental image of a woman in a burqa, her eyes emptied of kindness as she released the deadly weapon.

If we cannot identify the bomber, whom can we blame? Society needs to have someone to blame for the carnage and crimes committed against humanity. In cases where the female bomber was known, who were the most blameworthy of all? Culture? The men? The conflict? The state? Other countries?

Lisa continued, "We did a lot of things wrong in Afghanistan. We mistreated their homes and their property. Land and water are two important things for the people there, and we abused them."

Lisa experienced Afghanistan with unceasing love for its people. She sat with tribal men, one of whom had an emotional breakdown in front of her. She was given permission to meet the women behind the curtain, the wives of elders who had seldom "felt compassion from their husbands or children," she told me. Lisa gained the trust of a shaikh, who invited her into his home to meet his three wives and twenty-one children. Her memories of Afghanistan went beyond a mosaic of colors spiraling across a cobalt sky.

From the beginning, the most immediate question for me was how Afghan women can attain the most basic human rights when traditions argue against it. It surprised me that women were denied gender equality promised to them under Islamic law. For decades, patriarchs and powerful Islamists have defined women's roles in society, denying them the opportunity to contribute to their country's growth as well as their own individual success. Confined to puritanical Islam, women are at risk from violent extremist groups.

"Many women are enslaved by men," Lisa said. "Some turn violent. They are soul sick."

I stared at her. She had tried for years to unravel the hidden complexity of violence committed by Muslim women in a country governed feverishly by men. The bizarre unpredictability of women's lives ordered by religious and traditional rituals had always frustrated me. Despite its complicated history, Afghanistan had its heroines—police officers, journalists, film directors, underground teachers, doctors, actresses, pilots, and paratroopers, to name a few, who were redefining their country's political and social landscape.

The more time I spent with Lisa, the more details of her career she confided in me. She told me that she had interrogated hundreds of terrorist suspects, sympathizers, and seasoned professionals. In 2009, in a northern Iraqi city, Lisa questioned the wife of a terrorist leader. She described her to me as a local woman with a baby. For twenty-one days, every day, Lisa tried to talk to the woman, who was angry and desperate to escape prison. She cried for hours; she paced her cell; she recited scripture. "Are you going to talk to me?" Lisa asked every day; on the fifth day, she brought the prisoner a cup of tea. "I want to understand. Is this jihad?" The woman replied, "You killed my husband." Lisa made it clear that she wasn't going to hurt her.

"Some days, we said nothing," Lisa recalled. "Other days, she would talk to me, or I would hold her hand. The simple act of holding her hand let her know that she could trust me. I would keep my word. In exchange for valuable information, I would let her go, even though it was risky for her. If men knew she had been imprisoned and told us about them and their activities, they would likely kill her."

When the prisoner told Lisa everything she knew about the men, she was released. "We gave her $100 and sent her off in a taxi. We detained her longer than we should have. I remember the last conversation: she said al-Qaeda in Iraq was coming for her. I told her to escape, but ten miles down the road, extremist men stopped her and killed her. I regret her death, although she did the right thing by talking to us."

The conversations Lisa had with female extremists in Iraq would have been difficult in Afghanistan, where many women were unseen, unknown, and unheard of. Lisa wished she could have learned more about the bomber in Afghanistan who nearly killed her. To not know who they were made her feel anonymous and invisible. The survivors of suicide attacks might be, as writer Christopher Hitchens calls it in *Mortality*, "living dyingly," waiting for their own expiration date as night lacerates with bands of day.

Lisa found solace in the women of Afghanistan. She said, "What I know is that women have an amazing capability to secure each other. It's an emotional bond. We trust each other. I was supposed to hate these women because they are the enemy, but I know that's not always true. When you talk to women, you have a cultural exchange."

"Most women don't have decision-making power," I said.

"Men make false promises," Lisa added. "Their leaders tell them it's their duty to act; their children will be martyrs; they will go to Heaven. But we both know that not all women choose violence."

She continued, "We need to change the choices. Women have limited options in Afghanistan. I've seen women broken. They are caged. They are not nurtured by men. So, it's easy for men to psychically and psychologically abuse them; it's easy for men to control them. . . . The bond between men and women doesn't exist, as it does here [in the West]. . . . The loss of a woman means nothing."

*When women are manipulated, managed, and maintained by men, they are expendable.* I thought. *How does it end? Is it possible to break through the cycle of violence?*

"When does the violence end?" I asked.

"You start by listening," Lisa said. "I bring *me* to the job. I am a soldier first. I begin by asking Afghans, 'How can I help you?' We have to understand their side, and that's when listening helps. I lost two sons. I tell the tribes about my boys. It's genuine and honest."

Lisa understood that empathy demands authenticity, an acceptance of heart-numbing sadness expressed by a stranger. It is the desire for human contact, the ability to shift the perspective to the inside—empathy is the emotional consequence of sharing one's life story. For as long as I have known Lisa, she has given me the truest part of herself. She has made me proud to know her and helped me accept the banal truth that you can't have everything at the same time.

"I tell the men there is no life without women. Afghanistan needs men and women for progress," she said. The overstated truth of both genders working together for a common purpose—a strong, stable Afghanistan—should be the blueprint for American foreign policy. Without its women, Afghanistan will have no lasting peace.

"Ultimately, girls need an education," Lisa said.

The natural solution has always been education for girls. When they become wives and mothers, they pass on their schooling to the next generation. More important, the fundamental right to learning is a religious obligation. Islam grants girls the right to an education. In the time of the Prophet, women were granted access to him. He made special arrangements for the education and training of women, and some women in his family were the most knowledgeable on matters of faith. Ayesha was revered for her intelligence and scholarship of Islamic doctrine. She is believed to have reported more than two thousand traditions and set an example of women teaching women and men.

The importance of learning is highlighted in more than five hundred places in the Quran, beginning with the first commandment revealed to the Prophet through Archangel Gabriel: "Read in the name of your Lord, who created man from a clot. Read! And your Lord is the most generous. Who taught by the pen. Taught man which he knew not" (Quran 96:1–5). Scholars agree that this verse emphasizes the need for Muslims to learn and preserve knowledge with the help of a pen as well as the importance of record keeping for future generations. Like the Quran, oral traditions attest to knowledge as one of the greatest pillars of faith. The Prophet said, "Seek knowledge even if you have to go to China" and "God makes the path to Paradise easy for one who walks on it for gaining knowledge." Therefore, education is obligatory for women in the same way it is required for men. The fact that some Muslim countries refuse to honor the right to female education explains why women are underrepresented in politics, many fail to achieve economic independence, and most continue to live subordinated lives.

An Afghan-American scholar and activist, who wished to be unnamed, told me that progress for women is slow. In her briefings to the United States Congress, she focuses on improving the lives of women across Afghanistan. In one conversation, she confided, "It's getting worse for women. Whenever I go to Afghanistan, I see women suffering from violence, trauma, and abuse from their families. Even NGOs are taking advantage of these women by not providing adequate resources and support."

Afghanistan is slowly changing. In an interview, Herat's director of education, Ghulam Hazrat Tanha, once said, "If women are educated . . . their children will be too." According to a local religious leader, "Education is like sun and water. Without it, you can't grow anything. But if girls are educated, they can change our whole society."[4]

Lisa told me, "Today, some women in Afghanistan are educated and working. They are fighting for everything, but still submissive to the country's customs."

Outside, the sky had turned a faint rose color, the sun sinking, as I listened to Lisa's words, dark like the sea. I thought of all my Afghan friends, in and outside the city of Kabul, working toward a peaceful and prosperous Afghanistan. They know that terrorism is not over—that Afghanistan is open like a wound. A succession of leaders have tried, and failed, to secure the country. Over the past decade, the conflict brought out the worst in people: greed, corruption, great violence.

Nightfall set in. I wondered when Lisa might return to Afghanistan. If it was possible to find a civilized calm in a place haunted by unmarked graves. If, after retirement from the army, she would return to Afghanistan to find the women she once met when she was in uniform. If she might hear the collective fury of women expressed in poetry—the *landays*, or verses, of longing for love or a home and the truth about war—a secret form of rebellion that Afghan women used to share their heartbreak, shame men, and protest oppression committed against them. *My pains grow as my life dwindles; I will die with a heart full of hope.*

In Lisa's story, details of the female bomber were incomplete. I wanted to know more. But I knew that there is still much we do not know about the women in today's violent groups. To what degree do women participate in the various activities of the movements, such as recruiting new members, raising funds, or socializing the youth? The most important sequencing issue is when females join violent extremism: we barely have a glimpse into their lives, before and after they disappear into the fold of violent extremism. Some experts are still trying to understand the link between religion and extremism, a complex hybrid. While the role of women in violent extremism is no longer new, I continue to argue for further research to add depth to the analysis and undoubtedly uncover new questions.

In my living room, moonlight streamed in through passing clouds. It was getting late for Lisa, who had a long drive home. I wished we lived closer, to appreciate the intimate details of a person's life, the mercurial moods of a woman serving in the Muslim world, and the ghostly presence of lives swallowed by the earth.

"Every time I leave Afghanistan, I leave behind women who are not yet healed," Lisa said.

I knew the pain of having built another relationship with a woman in a faraway place, only to let it go, though her words and face would feel vivid for years to come.

"I come back home in tears," she said. "Every time. There's a closeness I feel to the place and the people. It's like a family bond that stays with me."

War makes death inevitable. As a researcher-storyteller, I cannot share Lisa's pain or know the signals of hurt that leave behind scars, the stories of suffering that pass like a slow-motion movie. Though I did understand the need to recognize that chronic social suffering is a fact of life. My mind will be forever stuck on the restlessness of not knowing if women will be free enough, and the need to answer this one urgent question: Will Afghanistan honor women's rights? No doubt this debate will rage, or splutter, for years to come: the never-ending cultural chasm between conservatives and liberals battling for a country to be kind to its women.

# PARADISE

There is no greater dream for a believing Muslim than the desire to enter Paradise. The ultimate goal is to breathe heavenly air and recline in gardens from which rivers flow, as the Quran promises, with a tribe of family, friends, and all of God's Prophets. How one achieves that dream is determined by actions in *this* life. A believer is told that the hereafter is for those whose acts of charity are stacked higher than the sins of a mortal. But the Afterlife, though an attainable goal, is not without the tests of faith that a Muslim endures on earth.

In an era of romantic terrorism, the rules for entry into Paradise are constantly rewritten, and a Muslim's rights and responsibilities are redefined. For nearly twenty years, I have witnessed the semantic folly that terrorists use to seduce seemingly innocent girls and women to resolve a grievance. For some women, the decision to join religious extremism is voluntary and is often driven by personal reasons, including the need to belong, to be loved, to be purposeful, and to offer a helping hand to a Muslim community suffering the barbarism of war.

Male terrorists use a gamut of tricks to lure women into their organizations and justify violence to vent frustration in a cause where dialogue and negotiation are nonexistent. Worse, terrorists flirt with the language of the Quran and a history of traditions to attract the attention of potential female recruits. The promise of Paradise is their greatest form of psychological warfare, with goals (the creation of a Muslim state) used to convince the vulnerable that violence is linked to the empyrean wonderland.

For nearly twenty years, I have lectured on the growing phenomenon of Muslim female extremists and highlighted four key points. First, the growing number of conflicts raging in the Muslim world gives girls and women few options for a secure future. With increased exposure to death, destruction, and violence, some females turn to violence as a natural response to effect change for their communities and countries. In the future, wars will continue to appeal to, attract, and have allure for women. Afghanistan is one of the many conflicts raging in the Muslim world. Beyond Afghanistan, there is violent opposition to rotten governments and vicious civil conflicts in the Middle East. These wars empower violent extremists and create unwieldy politics that struggle through painful processes of nation building. In many conflicts, women are caught between religious extremists and the state; cornered by cold-blooded conservatives; or ruled by families who appear indifferent, insensitive, and inflexible to their needs. The outcome of this struggle will dramatically shape the lives of women in the West and across the Muslim world.

Second, Muslim women drawn to long perspectives and political temporalities still have a personal motive. The different hypothetical possibilities of joining a violent group range from the rational to the absurd—to save the victims of war, the noble calling; or for marriage, motherhood, and martyrdom. To this end, violent men are persistent and offer women the illusion of a hopeful future entangled with unrealistic goals. Men play on a woman's emotions and use shame, guilt, humiliation, and injustice interchangeably to stress the importance of her commitment to Islam. Men use this tactic to prey on vulnerable women and convince them that they will find love, belonging, and purpose for their seemingly empty lives in extremism. Men entice women with the promise of Paradise, a pledge they cannot deliver. Only the Creator chooses who will enter His heavenly kingdom.

Third, beyond romance, some girls seek friendship and family. They need to connect with a global Muslim community. Their yearning for sisterhood and spiritual connection is their foundation, even when that connection is likely to be short-lived, superficial, and shallow.

Finally, ignorance of Islam and an overreliance on self-professed scholars encourages female recruitment. Without a proper understanding of the Quran, females are vulnerable to the perverted readings of scripture and oral traditions. It is common for extremist ideologues to engage the revelation without understanding the holistic tradition. In summer 2017, I taught a class titled Fatwa and Radical Islam to US government analysts and presented the extremists' view of the Quran as a linear book. I said what I know to be true of female and male extremists committing violent acts in the name of Islam: Extremists are ignorant of the deeper meaning of the sacred verses. They refute the need for introspection. The Quran says, "Verily, God does not change the conditions of a people until they change themselves." Extremists rebut thousands of respected scholars with knowledge of Islam. They renounce the universal principles of Islam that call for peace, love, mercy, compassion, and coexistence with *everyone.*

After nearly twenty years of teaching Islam, I have discovered that Islam is a simple, practical, and peaceful religion. Every year, I give a talk on Islam at a National Homeland Security Conference to emergency managers, law enforcement authorities, and military officers, and emphasize the significance and seriousness of *ijtehad*, literally "self-exertion" or "independent reasoning," which is derived from the word *jihad*, or "struggle." *Ijtehad* is a dynamic legal process by which scholars arrive at new interpretations to address contemporary needs. Whenever new issues are not explicitly addressed in the Quran or the Sunnah, the customs and sayings of Prophet Muhammad, scholars look at a history of previous rulings and reach a clear consensus on an issue. Only a qualified scholar has the right to declare a new legal ruling, or fatwa. Together, the body of fatwas comprises Islamic law, which is intended to be dynamic, fluid, and progressive.

Over the past decade, new scholars have emerged who are untrained and unlearned in the Quran. They have limited or no knowledge of Islamic history, culture, or jurisprudence. They dismiss other legal rulings on a similar subject. They have a superficial understanding of classical Arabic syntax, morphology, grammar, idioms, and rhetoric—all of which are necessary qualifications for a Muslim scholar. It goes without saying that extremists are degrading Islam's intellectual culture when they ignore the proper training and knowledge required to issue a fatwa. This is dangerous.

Extremist ideologues have ignored numerous fatwas *against* violence, arbitrary killing, and senseless war. Instead, they honor fatwas that justify killing and their right to enslave innocent women as well as take land by force. Undoubtedly, these illegitimate rulings are harmful to Islamic scholarship.

To counter religious extremists, moderate scholars and ordinary Muslims are speaking up against them. This gives me hope for the future of Muslim women. In September 2014, world-renowned Mauritanian Muslim scholar and professor of Islamic law Shaykh Abdallah bin Bayyah released a fatwa titled "This Is Not the Path to Paradise," drawing on Islamic history and scripture to reinforce the culture of peace in the Muslim heritage, a message that he said should be spread by the *ulema*, or scholars.

"The scholars are of utmost importance, as they are changing people's mentality by correcting concepts that have been misunderstood, and they play a great role in extinguishing the raging fires within the hearts and souls of so many. . . . If you don't defeat the ideas intellectually, then the ideas will reemerge," Bin Bayyah said.

In the same year, American-born scholar Shaykh Hamza Yusuf refuted ISIS and their idea of establishing a Caliphate in a recorded Friday sermon that is both powerful and evocative. Born Mark Hammon, Yusuf has a worldwide reputation for leading a movement to revive the Islamic spirit. In his talks, Yusuf reinforces the purification of the heart to cure spiritual diseases. Using textual evidence, he encourages Muslims to learn the "Quranic truth" through worship and a study of scripture. He often references this popular saying of the Prophet Muhammad: "You will never believe until you show mercy to one another."

In the end, extremism can never win a war. More and more Muslim countries and councils are coming together to issue new rulings to promote peace, mercy, and coexistence. In 2015, the

Senior Scholars' Council of Morocco issued a fatwa against terrorism after the Paris attacks—the legal ruling dismissed violence and coercion as alien to Islam. The same year, the Islamic Supreme Council of Canada issued a historic fatwa on joining ISIS; their fatwa became the first formal document to use Islamic law to debase the extremists' arguments for waging war. In 2016, hundreds of Muslim scholars gathered at the Promoting Peace in Muslim Societies forum, held in the pristine city of Abu Dhabi in the United Arab Emirates, to discuss misconceptions about Islam. Together, scholars dismissed the Caliphate as a legitimate political system in contemporary society and used this argument to debunk the extremists' justification for war.

In October 2017, the Women's Islamic Initiative in Spirituality and Equality (WISE), led by women's rights activist Daisy Khan, sponsored an event titled "Knowledge Ends Extremism" in Washington, DC. The one-day summit brought together hundreds of academics, scholars, religious and community leaders, policy makers, and others to prevent the spread of extremist ideology and hate crimes in America. Before the event, I spent time with Khan in her New Jersey home. At the dinner table, surrounded by her vast collection of books by Muslim saints, we slowly began to understand one another.

"I married the imam," she said proudly. Her husband, Imam Feisal Abdul Rauf, was away from home, touring his birth country, Egypt, with his new book, *Defining Islamic Statehood*. Listening to the story of her journey into Islam helped me appreciate our shared background and common experience with faith. We both have familial roots in Kashmir. We both came to America as immigrants, except that I arrived as a baby and she as a teenager. We both celebrated other religious traditions (Daisy had Christmas with the nuns of her school convent in Kashmir, while I was raised with my parents' Jewish, Christian, and Hindu friends). And we both came to Islam later in life with the help of a spiritual guide—the only difference is that she married her mentor. That night, over rounds of tea, we shared our stories of being a Muslim woman in America, the struggle of living true Islam in the midst of terrorist attacks, Islamophobia, and hate crimes.

I had first seen Khan on television as a participant in the Doha Debates in Qatar. She argued against the motion "Muslims are failing to combat extremism." On the TV program in front of thousands of viewers, Khan said, "Ordinary people have to take back the responsibility. I'm talking about the work I am doing. . . . I know many other efforts that are going on in the world that are really contributing to us pushing back extremism once and for all." I remember showing the program to my students in admiration of a Muslim woman from Kashmir who dared to speak for Muslims fighting violent extremism.

The next morning, we rode together from her home in New Jersey to her New York office, where she is the executive director of the Women's Islamic Initiative for Spirituality and Equality, a women-led faith-based grassroots organization created in 2005, committed to helping Muslim women achieve gender equality and human dignity.

Khan is not alone. Muslim women in other countries and communities are fighting for their rights, even as they risk their lives to protect their gender from absurd Islamic rulings and extreme interpretations of the Quran by conservatives and violent extremists. The hope is that when Muslim women learn and understand religious scripture, they will be able to demand what they deserve in Islam: *inclusion*. Knowledge of faith will enable women to educate the younger generation of girls, providing them with answers and an awareness of Islam to restore a strong sense of self, identity, and purpose in life. I firmly believe that a strong identity rooted in Islamic teachings, which are compatible with a Western lifestyle, will help women negate the immoral teachings of religious extremists.

These tectonic transformations are only beginning. Women's voices are needed to liberate themselves from the deeply ingrained cultural and religious biases in certain Muslim families and countries. In time, I trust that more women will support a strong culture of change. As more Muslim women speak up, the extremists' logic will no longer matter. I learned this obvious truth when I left the US government and traveled to Muslim communities and countries in order to find the invisible martyrs of extremism—

women hoping for happiness, harmony, and a home. I learned as much about myself as I did about the women trapped in violent organizations. I recognized the need for an empathetic conversation with and between Muslims in order to understand and forgive each other's limitations.

Once more I thought of destiny. Once more I tore myself apart looking for reasons to explain the extremists' acts of cruelty against ordinary citizens. Once more I felt that the conclusions I reached almost twenty years ago still stand the test of time. *Terrorism is personal.* Each woman's story is unique. Local contexts, cultures, and circumstances are critical motivators. Above all, a woman's choice to join terrorism is, in part, the result of a rewards system. *Martyrs without a doubt will go to Paradise.* The martyr's death is firewood for Islam.

What can we do to destroy violent extremism? While many experts agree that the burden lies with the Muslim world to counter terrorism, the West can help by channeling much-needed resources, financial aid, and development to alleviate some of the local grievances. Eroding the power of violent movements and support for extremists can largely be achieved by encouraging an open political system that includes active female participation, rebuilding civil society, legislating educational reform, accounting for human rights abuses, and abetting Muslim women's organizations. However, for any of these processes to take shape, the conflicts in the Muslim world must first end. Absent any resolution to the conflicts that resonate on the Muslim street, violence will remain the preferred course of action.

The Muslim world has an equal, if not greater, burden to bear. Since many female extremists come from Muslim-dominated families and societies, the governments under which these women live have a responsibility to their people to eradicate the conditions that lead to radical recruitment. The first step is the teaching of Islam. The responsibility falls first on Muslim scholars, who need to learn how to speak to women. "The goal is not to redefine Islam but to have a deeper acceptance of the role of religion in modern society. The problem is that scholars have failed to make Islam relevant to its members," one imam told me. Scholars also have a duty to encourage families and communities to respect a Muslim woman's choices and restore her access to education and employment. Of course, progress will not occur vertically. Change will be incremental, and ultimately it takes openness for societies to progress. Strong predictors of change are pluralism, education, open markets, reform, and respect for women.

At the heart of Islam are intention, innovation, and inclusion. As a child, I had no relationship with the Quran, which continued until my service to the US government and the military forced me to answer questions about the concepts of honor, jihad, martyrdom, Paradise, and much more. Teaching these concepts helped me overcome the guilt I carried for not learning classical Arabic when I was younger. Without a teacher, guide, mentor, or learned Muslim friend, I had to forgive myself for my own ignorance and eventually find a community of scholars to provide the resources and education that would empower me to understand the Quran.

If I was to identify the motives of extremist women, I had to separate the purest practice of Islam from its extreme and twisted version. I needed more than everyday casual explanations to recognize why some Muslim women choose the gruesome path to enter the next world. Years of study and interviews helped me create the simple formula I call the Three Cs to explain why women turn to violence. As I detailed in this book's introduction, they fall into one or more of these categories: culture, context, and capability. I have used this model to help general audiences understand the process of recruitment. Of course, a wide range of psychological factors also explain terrorist behavior, such as shame, envy, guilt, self-pity, stress, social withdrawal, insecurity, rape, regret, depression, revenge, loss, and trauma. Every extremist woman exhibits one or more of these symptoms for different reasons, and therefore her heart is poisoned by religious fury. So, while there is no single pattern or a one-size-fits-all formula, I have learned that certain indicators exist to better our understanding of female extremists.

One of those indicators is a weak or wounded heart. Research has shown that the vulnerable are the most susceptible to extremists' propaganda. This is where Islamic counseling can help women reconnect with the divine truth and strengthen their sense of self.

According to Islamic psychotherapy, the cure for a diseased heart is a purified soul. In Islam, the heart and the soul are interlinked and interdependent on one another for personal growth and reflection. It is the heart that connects the self to the divine through the soul. As the Quran says, "Those who believe and whose hearts are set at rest by the remembrance of Allah; now surely by Allah's remembrance are the hearts set at rest" (Quran 13:28). Both the heart and the soul are a part of the *nafs*, or the "self," and the Islamic science of the self is called *nafsiyyat*. The Quran offers more than 140 references to the nafs and descriptions on the development of the self: how to be in a successful relationship with oneself, with others, with the universe, and with God. When the heart is wounded, the self invariably suffers, which is where Islamic counseling and psychotherapy is a treatment that can be helpful to Muslim females considering or leaving religious extremism.

An important feature of Islamic counseling, unlike other therapy practices, is that it encourages an understanding of one's place in the world by focusing on knowledge of the universe and its signs: "And He is Who spread the earth and made it firm mountains and rivers, and of all fruits He has made in it two kinds; He makes the night cover the day; most surely there are signs in this for a people who reflect" (Quran 13:4). Thus, Islamic counseling moves beyond the realities of this world and works with what is *beyond the self* by emphasizing a spiritual connection. This therapeutic approach accepts and applies the significance of faith, especially for Muslims living in Western countries.

For years, as an adult, I received Islamic counseling to understand my own identity struggle and personal choices made for me by men. What I have learned is that Islamic counseling takes a holistic approach to healing the emotional, psychological, social, and subconscious self. Islamic counseling practices connect the afflicted Muslim to the divine truth and reorient followers to a more peaceful and more hopeful future that honors one's place in *this* world while being conscious of *that* world, the heavenly kingdom we call Paradise.

By comparison, Islamic counseling is similar to cognitive behavioral therapy, a model that other terrorism researchers and scholars, including UK-based Dr. Erin Saltman, firmly believe is the right treatment for radical Muslim women. In her London office, Saltman told me that she disliked the term *deradicalization*, a process by which a religious extremist changes behavior and beliefs and denounces the use of violence under the guise of Islam. Deradicalization is a concept largely accepted by US government officials and a wide group of scholars, whom I personally know, but this treatment is singular in approach and fails to account for a person's religious background.

Instead, Saltman prefers a therapy that helps people see the relationships between beliefs, thoughts, and feelings. As I have learned from her, cognitive behavioral therapy is grounded in a person's perception of events, rather than the events themselves, which determines how she will feel and act. When I was studying under Dr. Jerrold Post, a professor of psychiatry at the George Washington University, I was taught that individuals with emotional and behavioral problems had the most to gain from cognitive behavioral therapy because it can treat a wide variety of conditions, including anxiety, depression, posttraumatic stress, persistent pain, and anger-management issues. But unlike cognitive behavioral therapy, Islamic counseling encourages Muslims to reconnect to God in a peaceful, loving manner or to their final goal, Paradise.

I have often wondered how powerful this psychotherapy could be for other Muslim females struggling with their family, values, relationships, and God. In religious extremist groups, men often define a woman's position and place in this world, including her roles and responsibilities. In other words, women lose all rights when they resign their lives, and freedom, to the care of violent men. This is why I have argued that women are expendable, easily abused and used, and many are exhausted by serving the desires of men. Women will never be "whole," physically whole and emotionally together, when controlled by men or other radical women.

Ultimately, male extremists do not value Muslim women. They do not understand that women are not the custodians of their honor. When the Prophet of Islam glorified women, why are so many Muslim women oppressed? We know from numerous studies that some women choose violence as a sign of status, safety, or sanity. In doing so, they have negated Islamic history, which extols the first Muslim women for their piety, personality, and protection of Islam. Still, in the contemporary Muslim world, the oppression of women continues from the cultures and customs of violent men. Traveling to different parts of the Muslim world, I have learned that women have the power to stop this cruelty and delegitimize the extremists' false logic of Paradise. The good news is that more Muslim women today are calling for a purer practice of Islam and rejecting the most exclusionary and inequitable interpretations of their religion. The faithful know that extremists are manipulative and offer only a make-believe version of Paradise.

❀

In my home, I stand wrapped in a shawl by the balcony window and watch dollops of snow bleach the ground a silvery white. Finishing the writing of this book, I think back to the intimate stories of women willing to die for an ideal that is foreign to me. The catastrophic voices of female protesters in Kashmir still shatter me inside because they live in conflict. The ease with which women, or young girls, join religious extremism through an online platform, such as a website, chat room, or tweet, longing for Paradise is mind-numbing and frustrating. Details about the woman draped in black as she gunned down innocent victims in San Bernardino made me question the absurdity of her love for her extremist husband or the baby she abandoned when she turned to violence. *What kind of love is this?* I thought.

In the years since I left the US government, I have given hundreds of talks around the world to many different audiences on extremism and the role of women in Islam. The question I get asked most often is: Are you still hopeful? Everyone has read some horrific story of a woman strapped to a bomb, a female accomplice to an attack, or girls seduced online by male extremists. The answer to the oft-repeated question is a resounding yes. I am optimistic that violent extremism will be delegitimized and disgraced as more

Muslims study the Quran. As I've said throughout this book, a lived Islam is an important part of the solution. A faith-filled life offers a strong sense of self—the missing identity piece—and belonging that these girls and women are searching for. Knowledge of Islam frees women from the narrow rulings by violent extremists and hard-line conservatives—both are equally damaging to women's rights and limit their opportunities and choices. Without this knowledge, women will be subjected to and silenced by the patriarchy.

It had never occurred to me to tell this story of tragedies. The storytelling is accidental, and yet written for the sake of truth and for the teachers who believed that to hold back would be to deny life. As I write, my memories of female extremists are uneven. A part of me wants to forget their misadventures, but I know their stories can never be erased.

In an era of cultural sensitivity, I applaud the women strong enough to counter religious conservatives and extremists, both of whom encourage a limited role for Muslim women. Collectively, I believe that women of all faith traditions need to say that certain cultural and religious baggage will not be admitted. We already know that violent extremism is *haram*, or forbidden in Islam, and it is punishable by secular law. We already believe that women everywhere need to be protected from violent men, and many women I have met in my travels also understand that a sound education that respects all faiths and people is freedom from bigotry, prejudice, and extremist beliefs. That is a sign that as women, we too hold certain things sacred: among them equality, liberty, the pursuit of happiness, and the right to be. If only this basic truth had come to me much sooner in life. If only I had discovered the beauty of Islam and its women through the Quran, rather than the cases of violent women.

Since my years spent in the Counterterrorism Center, I have replaced my ignorance of faith with an almost complete reinvention of myself. For so long, my identity had been forged by my work in counterterrorism and the distorted versions of Islam, forcing me to question a woman's place in it. The nightmares that had forced me awake at night were replaced by a revival of faith. With a new attachment to the spirit of Islam, I was able to value ancient traditions and set my own expectations—to be a learned Muslim woman capable of denouncing religious extremism on the basis of faith.

Still, we live in an age of terrorism. The future, an alternative story, of women rising against violent men is already happening, though change can be glacially slow. One of my worst fears is that more women may choose violence and strive for a perversion of Paradise in which they become invisible martyrs, if *this* life is unbearable, unjust, and ungodly. As writer Alain de Botton writes in *On Love*, "Life is a skill that has to be acquired, like learning to ride a bicycle or play the piano."[1] For female extremists, it would take enormous skill to teach them that Islam is a balanced religion that abhors suicide, killing, and senseless war. They would need to believe that God created men and women from a single soul (Quran 4:1) and that women are equal to men in the eyes of God.

The more I learned about Islam, the more inclined I felt to share with female supporters of violence the fact that *this* life has to be lived in complete charity and service to humankind in order to enter the Afterlife. And yet, women who accept violent action make illogical and childish choices that Muslims with a deeper understanding of the Quran could not make. Therefore, learning how to live as a Muslim woman requires knowledge of faith, an educational tool that empowers, enlightens, and emboldens women against male extremists and toward a life with more hope, optimism, and purpose. Research shows that only the Islamic faith can provide "comfort, meaning, identity, spirituality, and community for its followers." Two factors, positive religious coping and intrinsic religiosity, were positively linked to a believer's mental health and well-being.[2]

Eventually, the snow stops and ice sheets sculpt the landscape. The coming and going of cold is evidence of time, the passage of seasons a symbol of something changing. I lift my hands up toward a pearl-gray sky, and in a quiet voice, I chant my mother's prayer: *Be constantly occupied instead with listening to God.*

Later that evening, I find an Islamic oral tradition that encourages Muslims to speak against injustice, insolence, and the irresponsible actions of extremists. The tradition reads, "The strongest of faith are those who take action."

Bless the activists. Bless the women with the courage to say no to extremism.

# NOTES

INTRODUCTION

1. USAID, *Guide to the Drivers of Violent Extremism*, February 2009, https://pdf.usaid.gov/pdf_docs/PNADT978.pdf.

2. Farhana Qazi, "The *Mujahidaat*: Tracing the Early Female Warriors of Islam," in *Women, Gender, and Terrorism*, eds. Caron E. Gentry and Laura Sjoberg (Athens, Ga.: University of Georgia Press, 2011).

3. Anna Erelle, *Undercover Jihadi Bride: Inside Islamic State's Recruitment Networks* (New York: HarperCollins Publishers, 2012).

CHAPTER 1

1. According to British author and historian Victoria Schofield, "What Radcliffe did was conform to the suggested boundaries [that had] already been worked out in February 1964 before the [British] Cabinet Mission arrived in India." Email correspondence, February 2015.

2. Joseph Campbell, *The Power of Myth* (New York: Apostrophe S. Productions, Inc., 1991), 25.

3. Yann Martel, *Life of Pi* (Canada: Harcourt Books, 2001).

4. Karen Armstrong, *Islam: A Short History* (New York: Random House, 2002).

5. Jeffry R. Halverson, H. L. Goodall, Jr., Steven R. Corman, *Master Narratives of Islamist Extremism* (New York: Palgrave Macmillan, 2013), 12.

CHAPTER 2

1. Mirza Waheed, *The Collaborator* (London, UK: Penguin, 2012), chapter 1.

2. "1st female suicide bomber hits Indian Kashmir, police say," *USA Today*, World, October 13, 2005, http://usatoday30.usatoday.com/news/world/2005-10-13-female-bomber_x.htm. Also see Swati Parashar, "*Aatish-e-Chinar*: In Kashmir, Where Women Keep Resistance Alive," in *Women, Gender, and Terrorism*.

3. Quoted in Parashar, "*Aatish-e-Chinar*: In Kashmir, Where Women Keep Resistance Alive," in *Women, Gender, and Terrorism*.

4. Qazi, "The *Mujahidaat*," in *Women, Gender, and Terrorism*, 30.

5. Mia Bloom, *Bombshell: Women and Terrorism* (Philadelphia: University of Pennsylvania Press, 2011).

6. Farhana Ali and Jerrold Post, "The History and Evolution of Martyrdom in the Service of Defensive Jihad: An Analysis of Suicide Bombers in Current Conflicts," *Social Science Research Journal* 75, no. 2 (Summer 2008): 619–20. (Published under my former name.)

7. Jessica Stern, *Terror in the Name of God: Why Religious Militants Kill* (New York: HarperCollins, 2003).

CHAPTER 3

1. Farhana Ali, "Dressed to Kill: Why the Number of Female Suicide Bombers Is Rising in Iraq," *Newsweek*, July 30, 2008.

2. Mia Bloom, "Women as Victims and Victimizers," eJournal USA, May 2007.

3. Haifa Zangana, *City of Widows: An Iraqi Woman's Account of War and Resistance* (New York: Seven Stories Press, 2007).

4. Fahimeh Fahiminejad, "Exemplary Women: Lady Umm Salamah," in *Message of Thaqalayn* 12, no. 4 (Winter 2012).

5. Anita McNaught, personal communication with the author.

6. Alissa J. Rubin, "How Baida Wanted to Die," *New York Times*, August 12, 2009, https://www.nytimes.com/2009/08/16/magazine/16suicide-t.html.

CHAPTER 4

1. Qazi, "The *Mujahidaat*," in *Women, Gender, and Terrorism*.

2. Farhana Ali, "Inside a Girls' Madrasa," *Washington Post*, March 2008.

3. For an accurate list of the Prophet's wives and notable women, see Mahmood Ahmad Ghadanfar, *Great Women of Islam: Who Were Given the Good News of Paradise* (Houston, TX: Dar-us-Salam Publishers, 2001).

4. Assad Nimer Busool, *Muslim Women Warriors* (Chicago: Al-Huda, 1995), 35.

5. Jennifer Heath, *The Scimitar and the Veil: Extraordinary Women of Islam* (Mahwah, N.J.: HiddenSpring, 2004), 215.

CHAPTER 5

1. Jesse Paul, "Colorado girls urged friends to pray for them as they headed to Syria," *Denver Post*, October 23, 2014, https://www .denverpost.com/2014/10/23/colorado-girls-urged-friends-to-pray-for-them-as-they-headed-to-syria/.

2. Rita Katz, "From Teenage Colorado Girls to Islamic State Recruits: A Case Study in Radicalization Via Social Media," *Insight Blog and Terrorism & Extremism*, November 11, 2014, https://news.siteintelgroup .com/blog/index.php/entry/309-from-teenage-colorado-girls-to-islamic-state-recruits-a-case-study-in-radicalization-via-social-media.

3. There are four waves of terrorism, according to a model created by a counterterrorism champion and scholar, Dr. David Rappaport, whom I met many years ago.

4. From "The Death of the Hired Man," by Robert Frost.

5. From "The House of Belonging," by David Whyte.

CHAPTER 6

1. Kirk Mitchell, "Arvada teen jihadist wannabe sentenced to four years in prison," *Denver Post*, January 23, 2015, https://www.denverpost .com/2015/01/23/arvada-teen-jihadist-wannabe-sentenced-to-four-years-in-prison/.

2. From a criminal complaint report signed by US Magistrate Judge Kristen L. Mix and signed by Christian K. R. Byrne, Task Force Officer, FBI-JTTF, Case No. 14-mj-01045-KLM, April 9, 2014, United States District Court for the District of Colorado.

3. Ibid.

4. Mitchell, "Arvada teen jihadist wannabe sentenced to four years in prison."

5. Vicky Collins reporting for ABC News on Shannon Conley's sentencing hearing, US Attorney's Office, Colorado, January 2015.

6. Michael Martinez, Ann Cabrera, and Sara Weisfeldt, "Colorado woman gets 4 years for wanting to join ISIS," CNN, January 24, 2015, https://www.cnn.com/2015/01/23/us/colorado-woman-isis-sentencing/; and Michael Roberts, "Shannon Conley, teen accused of trying to aid ISIS terror group: Her rebirth as "Slave of Allah," Westword, July 3, 2014, http://www.westword.com/news/shannon-conley-teen-accused-of-trying-to-aid-isis-terror-group-her-rebirth-as-slave-of-allah-5878186.

7. Steven Davy, "These Mothers Lost Their Sons to ISIS. A Photographer's Work Documents Their Pain," Public Radio International, April 19, 2016, https://www.wbez.org/shows/the-world/these-mothers-lost-their-sons-to-isis-a-photographers-work-documents-their-pain/677cdc3f-28e3-4d5d-88cb-38376eca29ba.

8. Victoria L. Dunckley, *Reset Your Child's Brain: A Four-Week Plan to End Meltdowns, Raise Grades, and Boost Social Skills by Reversing the Effects of Electronic Screen-Time* (Novato, Calif.: New World Library, 2015).

9. Nancy E. Willard, *Cyber-Safe Kids, Cyber-Savvy Teens: Helping Young People Learn to Use the Internet Safely and Responsibly* (San Francisco: Jossey-Bass, 2007).

CHAPTER 7

1. Joseph Campbell, *The Power of Myth* (New York: Apostrophe S. Productions, Inc., 1991).

2. Saniyasnain Khan, *Goodnight Stories from the Quran* (Birmingham, UK: Goodword Books, 2007).

3. Erin Marie Saltman and Melanie Smith, *Till Martyrdom Do Us Part: Gender and the ISIS Phenomenon* (Institute for Strategic Dialogue, 2015), https://www.isdglobal.org/wp-content/uploads/2016/02/Till_Martyrdom_Do_Us_Part_Gender_and_the_ISIS_Phenomenon.pdf.

CHAPTER 8

1. Carolyn Hoyle, Alexandra Bradford, and Ross Frenett, *Becoming Mulan? Female Western Migrants to ISIS*, Institute for Strategic Dialogue, 2015, https://www.isdglobal.org/wp-content/uploads/2016/02/ISDJ2969_Becoming_Mulan_01.15_WEB.pdf.

2. David Eagleman, *The Brain: The Story of You* (New York: Pantheon, 2015).

3. https://islamfuture.wordpress.com/2009/12/16/the-role-of-the-women-in-fighting-the-enemies/.

4. An excellent historical novel about the Prophet's wives is *Mothers of the Believers: A Novel of the Birth of Islam,* by Kamran Pasha (New York: Washington Square Press, 2009). For an accurate list of the Prophet's wives and notable women, see Ghadanfar, *Great Women of Islam.*

5. Busool, *Muslim Women Warriors,* 35.

6. Heath, *The Scimitar and the Veil,* 215.

7. Jon Henley and Vikram Dodd, "Kadiza Sultana: London schoolgirl who joined Isis believed killed in Syria airstrike," *Guardian,* August 12, 2016, https://www.theguardian.com/uk-news/2016/aug/11/london-school-girl-kadiza-sultana-who-joined-isis-believed-killed-in-syria-airstrike.

8. Lizzie Dearden, "Syria girls: At least 60 British women and girls as young as 15 have joined ISIS in Syria, police say," *Independent,* March 1, 2015, https://www.independent.co.uk/news/uk/home-news/syria-girls-at-least-60-british-women-and-girls-as-young-as-15-have-joined-isis-in-syria-10078069.html.

9. Ibid.

10. Kalsoom Bashir, "Observer Op-Ed: British Muslim girls and extremism: what I learned on my journey across the UK," *Inspire,* April 2, 2015, https://wewillinspire.com/british-muslim-girls-and-extremism-what-i-learned-on-my-journey-across-the-uk/.

11. Ibid.

12. Kalsoom Bashir, "Education is the cornerstone of our society," *Inspire,* September 9, 2005, https://wewillinspire.com/education-is-the-cornerstone-of-our-society-kalsoom-bashir/.

13. Ibid.

14. Rosie Kinchen, "I'm taking on the Islamists. But where's your backbone?" *Sunday Times,* September 4, 2016, https://www.thetimes.co.uk/article/im-taking-on-the-islamists-but-wheres-your-backbone-dsnbf0zqq.

15. Sara Khan and Tony McMahon, *The Battle for British Islam: Reclaiming Muslim Identity from Extremism* (London: Saqi Books, 2018).

16. Ahmad Bostan, interview with the author, 2016.

17. Laura Scaife, interview with the author, 2017.

CHAPTER 9

1.  From his novel *Requiem for a Nun*, 1951.

2.  Christina Lamb, *The Sewing Circles of Herat: A Personal Voyage Through Afghanistan* (New York: HarperCollins, 2002).

3.  Global Terrorism Index, Institute for Economics and Peace, 2017. In 2017, Afghanistan placed second after Iraq.

4.  From Isobel Coleman, *Paradise Beneath Her Feet: How Women Are Transforming the Middle East* (New York: Random House, 2013).

CONCLUSION

1.  Alain de Botton, *On Love: A Novel* (New York: Grove Press, 1993), 221.

2.  Hisham Abu-Raiya and Kenneth I. Pargament, "Empirically based psychology of Islam: Summary and critique of the literature," *Mental Health, Religion & Culture* 14, no. 2 (2010): 93–115.

# ACKNOWLEDGMENTS

I would like to thank the hundreds of people I have met during my travels, who gifted me their knowledge. They have allowed this book to be created. In my search for meaning, teachers and spiritual leaders have guided me with grace. My most heartfelt thanks go to Imam Sayed, Ismail bin Ali, Eric Selbin, Jerrold Post, Robert Young Pelton, and Shaykh Hamza Yusuf, whose lectures enlighten me.

I am very grateful to the many experts who have assisted me throughout this process, providing contacts, answering questions, reading sections of the manuscript, and helping in innumerable ways. My thanks to Betsy Ashton, Tanisha Tingle, Arifa Khaled, Amanda Ohlke, Brian Michael Jenkins, Maya Yamout, David Birdsey, Carol Adler, Ambassador Akber Ahmed, Erin Saltman, Ahmad Bostan, Lois Herman, Vicky Collins, Anita McNaught, Jennifer Parker, Isobel Coleman, and Melissa Arciero-Durr.

At Berrett-Koehler, Anna Leinberger was a gracious, patient, and encouraging editor. She and her team helped steer this draft with enthusiasm and offered insightful comments. Their persistence brought this book to fruition. Jill Marr, my agent, helped me with the publishing world. I am thankful for her assistance, steady hand, and loving support.

Finally, my greatest support has come from my children—bless you for your patience and understanding as I tell this story. And I need to give a special thanks to my sister, who shared my journey into Islam, asking the same questions; searching for identity, belonging, and meaning.

# INDEX

# ABOUT THE AUTHOR

© Southwestern University

Farhana Qazi is an award-winning speaker and scholar on conflicts in the Muslim world. Born in northern Pakistan and raised
in Texas, she straddles the East and West and brings multiple perspectives to her work. As a young analyst, she began her study of
violent extremism in the US government, where she briefed senior
policy makers and practitioners on the growing threat. Upon leaving government service, she continued her work as a researcher
and traveled to countries in the Middle East and South Asia to further understand the drivers of radicalization. As a senior instructor for the US military, she trained hundreds of men and women in
uniform on Islam, Pakistan, and global threats. Farhana is a recip-
ient of the 21st Century Leader Award, presented by the National
Committee on American Foreign Policy in New York, for her training and service to the US military, and she received the Distin-
guished Humanitarian Award from Southwestern University, her
alma mater in Texas, for her research on women in war.

Her first book, *Secrets of the Kashmir Valley*, is the story of wom-
en's survival, struggle, and sacrifice in the age-old conflict in Kashmir, a bowl-shaped valley situated between nuclear rivals India and
Pakistan. She is the founder of Global Insights, LLC, where she con-
ducts independent research on violent extremism, provides training on Islam and conflicts in the Muslim world, and works with
clients to resolve complex problems in conflict-prone countries. As

an expert, Farhana has appeared in mainstream media: CNN, the BBC, PBS, National Public Radio, Fox News, C-Span, Bloomberg, ABC News, MSNBC, Canadian national television, Voice of America, Al Jazeera, *The Daily Ledger*, and more. She is a graduate of the National Security Studies Program at the George Washington University and holds a bachelor of arts with a major in political science and a minor in French from Southwestern University in Georgetown, Texas. She lives in Virginia.

# Berrett–Koehler
## Publishers

Connecting people and ideas
to create a world that works for all

Dear Reader,

Thank you for picking up this book and joining our worldwide community
of Berrett-Koehler readers. We share ideas that bring positive change into
people's lives, organizations, and society.

**To welcome you, we'd like to offer you a free e-book.** You can pick from
among twelve of our bestselling books by entering the promotional code
**BKP92E** here: http://www.bkconnection.com/welcome.

When you claim your free e-book, we'll also send you a copy of our e-news-
letter, the *BK Communiqué*. Although you're free to unsubscribe, there are
many benefits to sticking around. In every issue of our newsletter you'll find

- A free e-book
- Tips from famous authors
- Discounts on spotlight titles
- Hilarious insider publishing news
- A chance to win a prize for answering a riddle

Best of all, our readers tell us, "Your newsletter is the only one I actually
read." So claim your gift today, and please stay in touch!

Sincerely,

Charlotte Ashlock
Steward of the BK Website

Questions? Comments? Contact me at bkcommunity@bkpub.com.